Cotherapy with Individuals, Families, and Groups

Cotherapy with Individuals, Families, and Groups

Edited by
Seymour Hoffman, Ph.D.
Sara Gafni, M.A.
Brurit Laub, M.A.

JASON ARONSON INC.
Northvale, New Jersey
London

This book was set in 11 point Bem by TechType of Upper Saddle River, New Jersey.

10 9 8 7 6 5 4 3 2 1

Library of Congress Cataloging-in-Publication Data

Cotherapy with individuals, families, and groups /
edited by Seymour Hoffman, Sara Gafni, Brurit Laub.
p. cm.
Includes bibliographical references and index.
ISBN 1-56821-316-6
1. Multiple psychotherapy—Case studies. 2. Paradoxical psychotherapy—Case studies. I. Hoffman, Seymour, Ph.D. II. Gafni, Sara. III. Laub, Brurit.
[DNLM: 1. Psychotherapy—methods. 2. Mental Disorders—therapy—case studies. WM 420 D5366 1955]
RC489.M85I56 1995
616.89'14—dc20
DNLM/DLC
for Library of Congress 94-20885

Manufactured in the United States of America. Jason Aronson Inc. offers books and cassettes. For information and catalog write to Jason Aronson Inc., 230 Livingston Street, Northvale, New Jersey.

Dedicated to our respective parents

Irving, ז"ל, and Gussie Hoffman

Moshe, ז"ל, and Chana, ז"ל, Gafni

Benny, ז"ל, and Bracha Rosenberg

Contents

Foreword ix

Preface xiii

Part I: Individuals

1. Two on One 3
2. Active-Interactional Cotherapy 15
3. Cotherapy with a Borderline Patient 21
4. Cotherapy with a Bulimarexic Patient 35
5. Indirect Treatment of Traumatic Experiences 45
6. Phantom Cotherapist 57
7. Cotherapy with an Iatrogenically Infantilized Patient 65
8. Cotherapy with a Phobic Patient 73

9. Intervention by a Consultant to Overcome Therapeutic Impasse 79

Part II: Families

10. Cotherapy with an Electively Mute Child 89

11. Cotherapy with a Case of "Matricide" 99

12. Cotherapy with Anorexic Families 109

13. Cotherapy with "Marital Phobia" 121

14. Marital Cotherapy 129

Part III: Groups

15. Group Cotherapy 137

16. Use of the TAT in Group Therapy with Children 141

17. Teaching Cotherapy 149

Credits 153

Index 155

Foreword

During the past several decades new approaches to psychotherapy have proliferated. Some of these are based on complex and sophisticated theoretical models and others are boldly proclaimed to be atheoretical. The many overall approaches to treatment and the innovative specific techniques used have been detailed in the clinical literature. As a result, the mental health practitioner now has at his disposal a plethora of general approaches and specific techniques. However, this markedly enlarged therapeutic armamentarium may at times be a mixed blessing. The embarrassment of riches is often overwhelming. It is also confusing, for the clinician must contend with far from clear guidelines for the choice of therapeutic modality. Moreover, one has the uneasy sense that while the advocates of each method of treatment have enthusiastically described their therapeutic successes, they may have been less conscientious in reporting their failures.

One positive result that has emerged from these developments is a movement toward greater therapeutic flexibility. Although the tendency to fit all patients into the procrustean bed of the treatment procedures of a particular school of psychotherapy is far from dead, the notion that one particular method of psychotherapy is sacrosanct and provides the solution for all problems is losing ground. Increasingly recognition is given to the importance of adapting the method of treatment to the needs of the patient rather than the patient to the method. While treatment planning remains more art than science, it is at least less often based on dogma.

Though therapeutic flexibility unfortunately at times may in practice be synonymous with catch-as-catch-can looseness, there has been considerable progress in the direction of a more refined pragmatic eclecticism. A synthesis of contemporary approaches to treatment remains out of reach, but more and more there have been serious attempts to discern the underlying commonalities among the various schools of psychotherapy as well as their real differences, and to examine the relative effectiveness of different approaches and techniques in the treatment of specific types of difficulties. Increasingly, also, there has been a readiness to modify or adapt therapeutic techniques in ways that widen their scope of applicability.

Some of the techniques that have come into usage in recent years have their roots early in the history of psychotherapy, notwithstanding their novel and even daring and revolutionary appearance. One of these is cotherapy, or simultaneous treatment by two psychotherapists working together. Alfred Adler described the use of a cotherapy in his child guidance work in the 1920s, and Moreno the use of a cotherapist as auxiliary ego in the 1940s, but this technique did not achieve general acceptance for many years. However, in the past two decades it has gained a great deal of popularity, and it is now widely used in group and family treatment and also at times in therapy with individuals. While, by definition, cotherapy involves two therapists working together, the ways in which they relate and may choose to interact with each other and with the patient or patients are many and varied. Cotherapy is a technique of treatment that is not necessarily tied to a particular theory or system of psychotherapy. Thus, it is a tool of considerable versatility that can be used in many ways and settings.

The editors of the present volume have shared with us their experiences in treating a wide range of clinical problems in a variety of settings with patients of different ages using an active interactional cotherapy approach. The book is divided into three sections dealing with cotherapy of individuals, families, and groups. The sections consist of clinical case reports of patients manifesting a variety of symptoms, diagnoses, and complaints including anorexia nervosa, borderline personality disorder, elective mutism, depression, phobias, and marital and family difficulties. These accounts of treatment reflect the noteworthy flexibility of the therapists and the techniques and interventions used are often creative, imaginative, and challenging. The results are frequently impressive, especially in light of the fact that they were generally accomplished in a relatively brief period of time, lending support to the editors' assertion that cotherapy adds to the richness and effectiveness of the therapeutic process.

The last chapter of the book describes an in-service course on cotherapy conducted by the editors for their colleagues. I heartily support their recommendation that clinicians from all disciplines be taught and trained to do cotherapy, since it is a highly effective therapeutic modality in treating individuals, families, and groups.

Lily Dimitrovsky, Ph.D.
Associate Professor of Psychology
Bar-Ilan University

Preface

Cotherapy is the simultaneous treatment of patients by two therapists working together. In the last two decades, cotherapy's popularity has increased, especially in the treatment of groups and families, and, to a lesser extent, individual patients.

In the professional literature, a considerable number of articles have appeared discussing the theoretical underpinnings of cotherapy (Rubinstein 1981), its advantages and disadvantages (Russell and Russell 1980), its use in teaching and supervision (Bernard et al. 1980), the relationship between cotherapists (Heilfron 1969), and the clinical application in various formats (Hoffman et al. 1990), among other topics.

Among the advantages and benefits of cotherapy are: (1) enhancement of the treatment process, (2) expansion of the fund of creativity available to the patients and the range of interventions, techniques, and treatment ideas that may be utilized, (3) transference is enhanced while countertransference is better controlled, (4) by complementing each other, the cotherapists compensate for individual weaknesses, (5) training of the less experienced by the more experienced cotherapist, (6) burnout is prevented, (7) a model of interpersonal relationship is provided, and (8) mutual supervision and feedback are immediately available (Gafni and Hoffman 1991).

There are those who may view the use of two therapists in treating patients as prohibitive, especially in today's climate of health-care cost consciousness. However, it has been our experience that cotherapy significantly shortens treatment time and therefore, in the long run, is economical.

In our active interactional cotherapy approach, two therapists simultaneously treat the same individual (couple, family, group) and take consistently opposing roles and views of the patient from the beginning phase of therapy until positive change has been realized (Hoffman et al. 1987).

One therapist is provocative and challenging, confronts the patient's maladaptive defenses, and expresses skepticism regarding his motivation and ability to change, while the second therapist is encouraging and supportive and emphasizes the patient's strengths and desire and ability to change. The former focuses on and reflects the pathological and regressive elements, while the latter, the healthy aspects of the patient's ego (Hoffman et al. 1987).

Somewhat similar approaches have been described in the family therapy literature (de Shazer 1977, Haber and Cooper-Haber 1987, Papp 1980, Sheinberg 1985), where the goal of the interventions is to present the dilemma of various family members in relation to the presenting problem and make explicit the covert rules governing change.

The above dialectical interventions can be viewed as

> treatment strategies that embody two antithetical moves in such a way that as the pendulum swings from one to the other, change forces are mobilized and resistance is neutralized. The term "dialectical" is used in its Hegelian sense, meaning that these interventions consist of two coordinated contrary movements that may be thought of as a thesis and an antithesis. Although sometimes the intervention aims at giving maximum power to one of the polar movements, at other times it aims at an emerging synthesis. [Omer 1991, p. 565]

In the above approach, one therapist may function as an affective partner to the patients, helping them to experience and expand their bound-up feelings while the second therapist may attend to thinking processes, helping the patients use their rationalizations to manage anxiety constructively. In this way, the cotherapists help the patients understand that they are both feeling and thinking persons, not one or the other, and that they can usefully integrate these aspects of themselves with their behavior (Treppa 1971).

In this approach, one therapist can assume the role of container and nurturer and focus on the fantasy aspects of life, while the other takes on the role of the taskmaster who emphasizes aspects of reality.

As a result of the open discussion and free exchange of ideas and impressions that take place between them in the presence of the client(s), the therapists provide a model for the patient with conflicting feelings and thoughts—to negotiate and more effectively integrate the divided parts of themselves.

These interactions also enable anxiety-provoking and threatening material and information to be introduced into the peripheral hearing of the client(s) without stirring up their early warning systems (Hoffman and Gafni 1984).

By virtue of their different personality makeups and behavior, and (preferably) gender, the cotherapists are able to provide different role models for the patients and an opportunity to experience two adults who are not always in agreement, interacting with each other in an open and constructive manner.

This approach, when coordinated effectively, promotes the externalization of internal conflicts and ambivalencies and therefore makes them more readily available for therapeutic work and resolution.

This approach is most effective with (though not necessarily restricted to) highly resistant, passive, and poorly motivated patients with limited insight and interest in treatment (especially traditional, long-term forms of psychotherapy) (Hoffman et al. 1987). It is also effective in emergency situations where strong and immediate interventions, impact, and change are required and in situations of therapeutic impasse.

In our clinical work with individuals, couples, families, and groups using a cotherapy approach, we have become convinced of its efficacy in adding to the brevity, flexibility, and richness of the therapeutic process.

The case studies in this volume describe the rationale and techniques applied by the cotherapists in treating, in various formats, patients of various ages, diagnoses, and presenting problems. The book is divided into three sections: cotherapy of individuals, families, and groups. In Part I, case studies are presented of the treatment of a suicidal college student, an iatrogenically infantilized patient, a woman with a borderline personality disorder, and a young woman with claustrophobia, among others. In Part II, the treatment of anorexia nervosa, mutism of a young girl, "marital phobia," and a case of "matricide" are presented. In Part III, this approach in group therapy with latency children and college students is described. Psychotherapists, irrespective of their theoretical orientations and backgrounds, will find many of the studies informative, interesting, and relevant to their clinical practice.

The editors wish to thank the publishers for their permission to reproduce the articles, their coauthors and cotherapists with whom they have worked productively over the years at the Rishon le Zion Community Mental Health Center and Bar-Ilan University Student Counseling Service, Betty Hoffman for her editorial assistance and Judy Cohen, Senior Production Editor, for her help and cooperation.

References

Bernard, H. S., Banineau, R., and Schwartz, A. J. (1980). Supervision–trainee cotherapy as a model for individual psychotherapy training. *Psychiatry* 43:138–145.

de Shazer, S. (1977). The optimist–pessimist technique. *Family Therapy* 4:93–100.

Gafni, S., and Hoffman, S. (1991). Teaching cotherapy: instructional and supervisory processes. *Journal of Contemporary Psychotherapy* 21 (4):285–289.

Haber, R., and Cooper-Haber, K. (1987). Paradox and orthodox: a cotherapy approach. *Journal of Strategic and Systemic Therapies* 6(2):41–50.

Heilfron, M. (1969). Cotherapy: the relationship between therapists. *International Journal of Group Psychotherapy* 19(2):366–381.

Hoffman, S., and Gafni, S. (1984). Active interactional cotherapy. *International Journal of Family Therapy* 6(1):53–58.

Hoffman, S., Kohener, R., and Shapira, M. (1987). Two on one: dialectical psychotherapy. *Psychotherapy* 24(2):212–216.

Hoffman, S., Laub, B., Levin-Keini, N., and Jim, S., eds. (1990). *Readings in Cotherapy: Clinical Application with Individuals, Families, and Groups.* Ramat Gan, Israel: Bar-Ilan University Student Counseling Service.

Omer, H. (1991). Dialectical interventions and the structure of strategy. *Psychotherapy* 28(4):563–571.

Papp, P. (1980). The Greek chorus and other techniques of paradoxical therapy. *Family Process* 19:45–57.
Russell, A., and Russell, L. (1980). The uses and abuses of cotherapy. *Advances in Family Psychiatry* 2:401–410.
Sheinberg, M. (1985). The debate: a strategic technique. *Family Process* 24:259–271.
Treppa, J. A. (1971). Multiple therapy: its growth and importance. *American Journal of Psychotherapy* 25:447–457.

Two are better than one for they get a greater return for their labor.

Ecclesiastes 4:9

PART I
Individuals

1

Two on One

SEYMOUR HOFFMAN, RACHEL KOHENER, AND MICHAL SHAPIRA

Two therapists treating one patient is an effective technique not only in dealing with therapeutic impasses but as a therapeutic technique by itself. Watterson and Collinson (1976), in surveying the literature, cited several reasons why cotherapy is more effective than one-to-one therapy with certain individuals. Included in their list were (1) it allowed the patient to relate and develop transference toward persons of both sexes (in the case of male and female cotherapists); (2) the patient can express feelings of love and hate openly to each therapist, respectively, without ambivalence; (3) the combined knowledge and experience of two therapists is greater than that of one; (4) two therapists can give alternating and greater empathic support than one therapist alone; and (5) extreme dependency is less likely to develop.

Several authors (e.g., Dryud and Rioch 1953, Piaget and Serber 1970) view multiple therapy as an adjunct to individual therapy, its major advantage being its power to overcome therapeutic impasses.

Whitaker and colleagues (1956) suggested that cotherapy is more effective than one-to-one therapy with patients who fear overdependence or rejection or whose therapists have lost the conviction that the patient is treatable and regard multiple therapy as the preferred treatment with psychopaths and psychotics.

Piaget and Serber (1970) found that with their multiple-impact therapy technique (where from four to eight therapists participate), certain patient types, such as chronically resistive patients and passive dependent patients with specific "here-and-now" problems, who do not respond well to assertiveness training, are better prognostic cases.

Treppa and Nunnelly (1974) concluded that the distrustful patient, the patient with identity problems, the deprived patient, and the emotionally labile patient, benefited particularly from multiple therapy.

The tendency of a patient to assign roles of one kind or another to the therapist is well known. Individual therapy can result in ambivalence within a patient regarding the unconscious interpretation of the therapist role. The ability to separate and fuse good and bad images is frequently beyond the capacity of the patient, especially the more disturbed one.

Woodbury (1967), writing about the treatment of schizophrenic patients, makes the point that in a close relationship they are unable to entertain good and bad feelings toward the same person at the same time, nor can they tolerate mixed feelings in the same person. In Woodbury's terms, schizophrenics are only capable of a "univalent," as compared with the more normal "polyvalent," relationship. It was found helpful in their treatment to have two therapists so that the patients could better understand their contrary feelings and express them without disrupting the relationship.

The presence of two therapists, besides enabling the patient to "split" ambivalent feelings toward them, can provide support and give expression to the patient's regression while providing control and demands for responsible involvement with others (Mullan and Sanguiliano 1964). One therapist may deal with primary process material and fantasies while the cotherapist focuses on secondary process content and reality (Framo 1965). One therapist may confront while another may support the patient's defenses. One therapist can facilitate an explicit expression of the patient's conflicts, while the other therapist can facilitate its resolution. The latter can help patients identify ambivalent feelings, appreciate the impact of their behavior, and support patients' constructive behavior in relation to themselves and others (Treppa 1971).

The two therapists can also perceive and respond to the affective and cognitive aspects of the patient. While one may help the patient experience and expand bound-up feelings, the second therapist may encourage constructive reasoning (Treppa 1971).

Cotherapists may personify, represent, and reflect in a consistent manner patients' ambivalent feelings and perceptions of themselves and of others (Hoffman and Gafni 1984, Chapter 2, this volume).

Finally, two therapists, by virtue of different personality makeups, provide different role models for the patient and an opportunity to experience two adults, who are not always in agreement, interact with each other in an open, mature, and constructive manner.

It has been our experience that cotherapy with certain patients, especially if carried out in a highly active, and collaborative manner can facilitate change and psychological growth in a relatively short period of time (Hoffman and Laub 1986, chapter 10, this volume). This approach is most effective with (though not necessarily restricted to) highly resistant, passive-dependent patients with limited insight, motivation, and interest in prolonged and more traditional forms of psychotherapy.

In our approach, one therapist reflects the patient's "minuses" (fears, weaknesses, tendency to avoid coping with problems, and difficulty and resistance to changing lifelong habits) while the other therapist reflects "pluses" (hidden resources, strengths, achievements, and strong desire to change). In this way the patient is confronted in a direct, quick, and clear manner with ambivalence, conflicting feelings and contradictory behavior. One therapist is supportive, encouraging, and optimistic while the other is provocative, skeptical, and pessimistic regarding the patient's ability to change and grow. The latter attacks the patient's ineffective and maladaptive defenses while the former strengthens the healthy aspects of the patient's ego (Laub and Hoffman 1987, chapter 11, this volume).

Following are two case illustrations of the above approach.

Case Illustration 1

The patient, a 40-year-old bachelor, presented with complaints of depression, impaired concentration, and obsessive thoughts. He described himself as a quiet, reserved, and sensitive person who attempts to get along with everybody. He assiduously avoids conflicts and arguments and generally submits to people's requests for fear of offending them. As a result, he is an easy prey to exploitation.

The patient is highly vulnerable and readily affected by the topic of death and when exposed to news of death (radio, TV, death notices, etc.) he becomes depressed. For this reason, he avoids reading newspapers, watching TV, or visiting hospitals and sick people. When in the presence of mourners, he immediately distances himself and afterward bathes and washes his clothing because of his fear of contamination.

The patient is saddled by a low self-image, inferiority feelings, and superstitious beliefs.

As a child, he remembers being very sensitive, avoiding rough play and fights, and generally keeping to himself. He was excused from army service because of family reasons, which was fortunate for him because of his pacifistic beliefs and inability to harm anyone. His father died 20 years ago, and he lives with his "strong and dominating" mother and spinster sister.

The patient's outer demeanor reflected diffidence, anxiety, and insecurity, which contrasted sharply with his height and body build. He avoided eye contact, spoke sporadically and in a hesitant manner, and generally communicated the impression of apologizing for existing.

Treatment Interventions

In the initial interview conducted by the authors (male psychologist and female social worker) the patient seemed to be discomfited by the presence of the latter. However, with some encouragement and support he agreed to be interviewed by the two therapists.

After the intake, the therapists decided to see the patient together for several reasons: (1) the patient's difficulty in relating to women; (2) the patient's uneasiness and fear of psychotherapy (talking, exposing himself, exploring his past experiences and present emotions); and (3) his desire for immediate, concrete results.

Our assumption was that an active cotherapy approach, with emphasis on concrete tasks, here and now, and with a focus on specific goals, would produce more immediate and significant results. We decided to work with the patient on assertiveness because of the connection between this lack in his personality makeup and his various difficulties and complaints (death phobia, fear of confrontation, poor self-image, absence of self-confidence, and general feeling of impotence). We assumed that increased self-confidence and assertiveness would have a positive effect on his obsessive preoccupation with and fear of death and on his general functioning, as death is the most extreme example of impotence.

Following are several examples of the cotherapists' collaborative interactions in the treatment sessions.

> In the second meeting, the male therapist, in a provocative manner, asked for the patient's watch, since his own was old-fashioned and he had always wanted to possess a digital watch. The patient, with considerable embarrassment and uneasiness, complied with the request in spite of the cotherapist's attempt to persuade him to reject the request. The patient explained that since the psychologist desired the watch he was willing to part with it. The social worker encouraged the patient to demand the return of his watch, insisting that it wasn't *chutzpah* (nerve) on his part but his legitimate right. With considerable urging and encouragement, the patient garnered enough courage and succeeded in reclaiming his possession.
>
> In another session, the patient arrived depressed and related that he will have to move, the reason being the complaints of his neighbors regarding the dripping of his wash on their newly built patio. After a lengthy discussion about his feelings, options, and difficulties regarding the situation, the female therapist insisted that he was able to deal with the situation and was even able to hang his wet wash three times a week instead of twice to demonstrate his resolve. The cotherapist expressed skepticism and doubt that he was capable of doing this, pointing to the patient's tendency to run away from conflict rather than deal with it and suggested that he start looking for another

apartment. In the following session, the patient reported with great satisfaction that he had succeeded in the assigned task and received congratulations from the therapists.

At the end of the following session, the therapists by prearrangement raised the issue of when to schedule the next meeting. The male therapist preferred a later hour, but his colleague insisted on an earlier hour, and after some give and take, they reached a compromise. The patient was very attentive throughout the discussion, and at the end inquired from the female therapist if she weren't being too stubborn and inconsiderate. She responded that she was only insisting on her rights, and the cotherapist supported her.

In the next session, the cotherapists asked the patient to arrive at an earlier hour for the next session, the purpose being to cause him to request permission from his boss to leave early, something that he had never dared to do. Again the female therapist insisted that he was able to do this task, while the male therapist expressed strong doubts. At the following meeting, he arrived slightly late since he had asked to leave work a half hour rather than an hour earlier as requested by the therapists, and he apologized for his tardiness. However, the therapists praised him for having the courage to ask his boss to leave early, and the male therapist expressed admiration and surprise that he was capable of such behavior.

Treatment Outcome

The patient was seen eight times during a period of three months because of the planned departure of the female therapist from the clinic. During this period, noticeable changes were evident in his behavior and relationship toward the therapists. He appeared more relaxed, maintained eye contact, spoke more spontaneously and confidently, and on several occasions even challenged the views of the therapists.

In regard to his functioning outside the office, the patient reported that he felt more relaxed at work, more confident in social situations, more assertive at work and at home, and began dating a young woman on a consistent basis. The patient's depression and obsessive thoughts and fears regarding death and related issues significantly decreased, and he was again able to read newspapers and watch TV.

In a follow-up session conducted by the male therapist two months later, the patient reported that he was maintaining the gains achieved from the sessions but found it difficult to make further changes and to progress without help. He felt that he needed more "booster shots" and requested further sessions with the same format. His request was granted.

Discussion

The two therapists, working in this manner, were able to reveal to the patient his self- and public image. On one hand, the patient feels weak, impotent, cowardly, with a strong need to please and appease others, while on the other hand, he needs to prove that he exists, is worthwhile, potent, and capable of acting upon and influencing his environment and fate.

The provocative behavior of one therapist jolted the patient from his general malaise and passivity, while the encouragement and support of the other therapist enabled him to take constructive steps to change and improve his behavior and condition.

Also, the various interactions and behaviors demonstrated by the two therapists provided positive role models for the patient that he could both identify with and emulate (assertiveness, compromise, flexibility, expression of affection and anger within boundaries, sense of humor, openness, etc.) outside the treatment room.

Case Illustration 2

> Tami, a 10-year-old chubby girl, was referred to the clinic after being treated by the school psychologist for a year with no apparent improvement. Several years ago, after undergoing a psychological evaluation, she was transferred to a learning-disabilities class.
>
> The presenting problems included difficulties in concentration and attention, poor self-image, infantile behavior, and learning problems.

In our initial meeting with Tami and her family, which consisted of highly ambitious, successful parents and a 14-year-old brother, we were impressed by the warmth and concern of the parents and the passive and uncooperative behavior of the child. Tami was poorly groomed and dressed, displayed little interest in the discussion taking place, and on several occasions, left the room for brief periods of time.

The child's parents claimed that Tami was an intelligent and capable child and expressed strong reservations about her being in a special class. At their request, another psychological evaluation was done, and the results of this second evaluation indicated that Tami was of at least average intelligence. No evidence of organicity was found. The child's effort and involvement throughout the testing situation was minimal, although she did respond positively to urging and encouragement.

Tami's graphomotor productions and associations were revealing and provided the therapists with direction for the continuation of treatment. The child drew a tree with a nest of birds in it and gave the following story. "The mother and father birds do not leave their child alone. She doesn't yet know how to fly. She learns slowly. She has difficulty. One time the parents hid and the baby bird flew alone. She didn't know that they were looking."

In the therapists' view, this story reflected the child's intense ambivalence and the reason for her symptomatic behavior. On one hand, Tami enjoyed a certain comfort about her present condition and feared and resisted change, while on the other hand, she had a strong desire to change, progress, and display her abilities. On one hand, she absorbed the latent message of her parents (especially from the mother) to remain an infant in order to ensure the continued supply of maternal nurturing, while on the other hand, she was being continuously bombarded by their manifest message to grow and cope with life's demands in an age-appropriate manner. These mixed messages produced a great deal of confusion in the child and intense ambivalent feelings toward the mother.

In light of the child's passive-aggressive, resistant, and negativistic behavior to therapy, it was decided to see her individually and use an approach in which the two therapists would reflect in a consistent, concrete, and extreme manner Tami's ambivalence about how she saw and wanted to see herself and the mixed messages of her mother. The male therapist presented the regressive aspects of Tami, the advantages of being a little child (a lot of attention, few responsibilities, etc.). He also pointed out that to act like a "grown" child would require her to attend class regularly, pay attention, do homework, socialize with her peers, and be more independent—tasks that were beyond her capabilities.

The female therapist, on the other hand, insisted that Tami was a normal child and that if she wanted to, Tami was able to show people that she could behave in a mature manner. She pointed out that her present situation disgusts her and that she really wants to make friends, be more attractive, and be treated as a normal and mature child. The therapists argued their points in front of the child and made a bet as to who would prove to be right.

The female therapist expressed the opinion that Tami was capable of functioning in a regular class and received the child's permission to arrange with the school authorities to have her placed in a regular class but in a lower grade. The male therapist, however, doubted that she could function in a regular class after being in a special class for several years and predicted dire consequences. These remarks visibly offended and angered the child.

Treatment Outcome

In the fifth session, one was able to see changes in the outer appearance of the child. She had lost weight, had her hair curled, and wore a pretty dress. Tami reported to the therapists with great pride about her successful efforts in dealing with her studies and new classmates. The female therapist praised her lavishly while the male therapist, after grudgingly handing over the amount of the bet to his gloating colleague, insisted that although he saw some small changes, he was certain that she could not continue in this manner because of the immense difficulties and challenges awaiting her.

In the tenth and last session, the entire family was present. The parents reported that Tami was doing well academically and socially, was paying more attention to her appearance, and was much closer to them. At this point, Tami asked the male therapist if he really believed that she was not capable of behaving more maturely. The therapist responded that this had been his opinion in the past, but now he was not sure.

In a follow-up session with the family six weeks later, the parents reported that Tami was continuing to make progress in all areas. The child again turned toward the male therapist and asked him if he still had doubts about her. The therapist responded that now he was convinced that he had erred, and he apologized for his lack of faith in her.

Before departing, the parents warmly thanked the therapists for giving them a "new child."

Discussion

In this therapeutic approach, the child was able to direct hostile feelings to the "bad" therapist, while accepting support from the "good" one (different images of the mother). With these projective identifications, corrective experiences facilitated fusing them into a new representation of mother with whom the child developed a warm and communicating relationship (Solomon and Morrison 1972).

It is important to note that the therapists did not change their basic stance during the treatment even when some positive changes appeared. The theory was that as long as the ambivalence and maladaptive mechanisms were still in existence, their presence had to be acknowledged and reflected and alternative behaviors suggested. When the "provocative" therapist felt reasonably certain that the new behavior was sufficiently stabilized, he was then able to "join" his cotherapist and thereby reinforce the child's newly formed positive self-image.

Conclusions

Cotherapy with one patient can facilitate change and growth in a relatively short period of time. The approach enables the patient to more quickly and effectively become aware and come in contact with the "divided self" and make appropriate cognitive, perceptual, affective, and behavioral changes.

References

Dryud, J. E., and Rioch, M. J. (1953). Multiple therapy in the treatment program of a mental hospital. *Psychiatry* 16:21–26.

Framo, J. L. (1965). Rationale and techniques of intensive family therapy. In *Intensive Family Therapy*, pp. 143–212. ed. I. Boszormenyi-Nagi and I. L. Framo. New York: Harper & Row.

Hoffman, S., and Gafni, S. (1984). Active interactional cotherapy. *International Journal of Family Therapy* 6(1):53–58.

Hoffman, S., and Laub, B. (1986). Paradoxical intervention using a polarization model of cotherapy in the treatment of elective mutism: a case study. *Contemporary Family Therapy: An International Journal* 8(2):136–143.

Laub, B., and Hoffman, S. (1987). A multimodal psychotherapeutic approach to a case of "matricide." *Family Therapy* 14(1):35–42.

Mullan, H., and Sanguiliano, I. (1964). *The Therapist's Contribution to the Treatment Process.* Springfield, IL: Charles C Thomas.

Piaget, G. W., and Serber, M. (1970). Multiple impact therapy. *Psychiatric Quarterly (suppl.)* 44:114–124.

Solomon, A. P., and Morrison, D. A. R. (1972). Anorexia nervosa. Dual transference therapy. *American Journal of Psychotherapy* 26(4):480–489.

Treppa, J. A. (1971). Multiple therapy: its growth and importance. *American Journal of Psychotherapy* 25:447–457.

Treppa, J. A., and Nunnelly, K. G. (1974). Interpersonal dynamics related to the utilization of multiple therapy. *American Journal of Psychotherapy* 28:71–84.

Watterson, D. J., and Collinson, S. (1976). Copsychotherapy of the individual patient: indications and operative factors. *American Journal of Psychotherapy* 30:608–622.

Whitaker, C., Malone, T. P., and Warkentin, J. (1956). Multiple therapy and psychotherapy. In *Progress in Psychotherapy*, vol. 1, ed. F. Fromm-Reichmann and J. Moreno. New York: Grune & Stratton.

Woodbury, M. A. (1967). Object relations in the psychiatric hospital. *International Journal of Psycho-Analysis* 48:83–87.

2

Active-Interactional Cotherapy

SEYMOUR HOFFMAN AND SARA GAFNI

A considerable amount has been written on cotherapy and its advantages and effectiveness in working with both natural and artificial groups (Gans 1962, McGee and Schuman 1970, Napier and Whitaker 1978, Rabin 1967). The advantages cited are enhancement of the treatment process, support of the other therapist, and the training of a less experienced by a more experienced cotherapist (MacLennan 1965). In regard to treatment, transference is enhanced; counter-transference is better controlled; the family setting is re-created; identification is facilitated, especially when male and female therapists are paired; a model of interpersonal relationships is provided; a more objective basis for evaluation and diagnosis is developed (Holt and Greiver 1976), and mutual supervision and feedback ("covision") are immediately available.

The presence of two therapists enables one therapist to play a supportive, protective role toward the clients while the other can play an incisive, provocative role or, as Whitaker (1977) described it, one provides the anesthesia and the other performs the surgery. Also, two therapists form a bilateral participant/observer, and as one therapist holds back and observes, the other actively participates on an emotional level (Napier and Whitaker 1973).

For two people to work effectively together, they have to get to know each other and feel comfortable working together. There also has to be mutual respect, trust, and appreciation, and each must be forthright, flexible, and accommodating to the other in the working situation. Jealousy, competition, lack of respect, and incompatibility between cotherapists is a sure guarantee of disastrous results (Heilfron 1969, McGee and Schuman 1970).

While cotherapists may share their feelings and thoughts with clients and generally discuss the therapeutic sessions with each other afterward, little interaction occurs between them in the therapeutic situation itself. This we feel is unfortunate as it limits the potential of two therapists working in unison to effect growth and change in their clients. In this chapter we describe an approach we use at our clinic when working with couples and families. We call it the active-interactional approach.

In this approach, the therapists interact with each other and with their clients. They think aloud and share their views, feelings, and perceptions in front of clients; model selective behavior; role play; intentionally take identical or opposing sides on issues; and participate in paradoxical interventions. Beyond the already reported techniques of mirroring and modeling (Hannum 1980), cotherapist interactions mimic, replicate, reenact, and dramatize to make conscious a family's or couple's submerged rules and patterns of regulating behavior, and articulate the conflicts and inconsistencies. These techniques, we believe, help expedite change as they contribute to the demystification of therapy and narrow the felt gap between client and therapist, thereby enhancing the former's self-image. They also focus on the "here-and-now" reality in a more meaningful and effective manner and facilitate the bringing up of issues, dynamics, resistances, and conflicts more quickly for examination and resolution. What seems to take place in these interactions is a complex of two parallel processes: an emotional experience that emanates from the therapeutic interventions, and a cognitive one where clients can observe and compare their perceptions, views, and feelings with those of therapists.

A characteristic exchange occurs when one therapist seeks to co-opt his partner as a sounding board for interpretation, that is, introducing new information into the peripheral hearing of the clients without frontally threatening them. This allows for novelty of perspective to be aired by therapists, and is assimilated indirectly or subliminally by clients. As a technique, it circumvents a direct affront on defended and impermeable boundaries, hence avoiding client early warning mechanisms of resistance. This insinuation of new information into the clients' system plays on the suggestive and enjoys the surprise of indirect discourse.

As an illustration, therapist A says to therapist B in the clients' presence: "I guess you've probably got the feeling that we inadvertently touched a nerve when we asked about the in-laws. I don't think it's appropriate at this time to go into it—it's too delicate a matter. . . ."; or "I feel we're stuck and I don't think we can progress unless some change or movement occurs in their relationship. However, I don't think they're sufficiently interested in getting out of the morass they're in. . . ."

Cotherapist interactions along these lines are especially effective with resistant, passive-aggressive, and withdrawn clients. Through their dialogue, the cotherapists can raise issues, confront pathological behavior and dynamics, interpret behavior, and so on, without the clients' active cooperation, and also provoke them to participate in therapy.

To further illustrate the active-interactional approach we offer several anecdotal examples.

Case One

> A husband who was pathologically obsessed with his wife's sexual past and suspicious of her present sexual behavior, complained that while speaking to a male friend of theirs, she placed her hand on his knee. This he felt was sexually provocative while she insisted it was just her way to get his attention. At that point, one of the therapists moved her chair next to her co-worker's nonchalantly placed her hand on his knee and inquired, "You mean like this?" The wife did not answer, but followed the rest of the discussion with rapt attention. The husband was taken aback by the therapist's gesture and did not pursue it. He went on, however, to complain about his wife's immodest mode of dress (she then wore a short, tight skirt that exposed her thighs). The male therapist supported the husband with the comment that he would also feel upset if his wife's thighs were exposed in mixed company, to which his co-

worker nodded in agreement. In this fashion, the therapists working together supported and strengthened the healthy and reality-based perceptions and challenged and weakened the pathological and distorted ideas and behaviors of each partner.

Case Two

During a family session, the husband angrily interrupted his wife's complaints by saying, "But honey, that's not true. . . ." (Though the sessions were conducted in Hebrew, he spoke in his mother tongue.) The American therapist turned to his Israeli colleague and explained that "honey" was "*dvash*" in Hebrew. To this the latter remarked with a quizzical look on her face, "Oh! By the expression on his face, I thought he was addressing her as '*hometz*' [vinegar]." The wife explained that her husband always denied that he was angry even though it was evident to all that he was. The therapists then began discussing between themselves the husband's dynamics. One therapist pointed out that the husband had a tendency to deny his anger by sugarcoating it while the other observed that he expressed it in an indirect and passive-aggressive manner. They gave examples to support their contentions such as his refusal to bathe regularly and his tendency to dress like a slob, much to the embarrassment of his wife. In this fashion, the therapists working in tandem were able to cut through the client's resistance and begin working with an important dynamic early in treatment.

Case Three

An adolescent boy who was referred to our clinic because of truancy and stealing, was seen alone after several family sessions. It was felt that his father's presence was inhibiting him and that he would welcome an opportunity to speak in private. However, after his passive, detached behavior continued in the individual session, the cotherapists initiated a dialogue between themselves, attempting to mimic a conversation between the boy and his father. After several minutes, the boy interrupted the therapists by pointing out that his father would never react in such a mild manner. He was then invited to demonstrate, and continued the role playing with one of the therapists reacting to his "father" as he wished he could in real life. In this manner the boy came to recognize and acknowledge his pent-up anger toward his father and the indirect passive-aggressive expression of it via stealing and truancy.

Case Four

In a joint session, the husband related an incident where his wife had asked him to accompany her to the bathroom because she was afraid to go alone. (This occurred after she saw a frightening TV program.) He angrily refused and much tension arose between them. The male therapist remarked to his cotherapist that it would also anger him if his wife acted like a little child, thereby identifying with and giving support to the husband. The female therapist, in contrast, empathized with and supported the wife: "If I were in her place I would have been very angry, because if I had had to make such a request, it would be a sign that I was very afraid." The therapists, by identifying with and supporting each spouse, were able to help the couple better appreciate what was being experienced and communicated to them by their partner in life.

Case Five

A 10-year-old boy was brought to the clinic by his parents because of immature behavior and encopresis, which began several months following the birth of a sibling. After several sessions, one of the therapists declared that the child, because of his emotional immaturity, was not capable of controlling his bowels and therefore must be treated according to his emotional and not chronological age. This meant diapers, limited privileges, restrictions, etc. The child vehemently protested and insisted that he was capable of sphincter control, to which the therapist scoffed. A discussion followed between the cotherapists, whether the child was capable of controlling his bowels or not. The female therapist, expressing a more optimistic opinion, insisted on giving the child a chance to prove himself before implementing the new approach, to which the male therapist grudgingly agreed. The child returned the next session with a chart indicating a significant decrease in "accidents" and a triumphant expression on his face, much to the "chagrin" of the "pessimistic" therapist. By "joining" with the child against the "mean" therapist, the "kind" therapist was able to induce behavior change in a relatively short period of time.

References

Gans, R. W. (1962). Group cotherapists and the therapeutic situation: a critical evaluation. *International Journal of Group Psychotherapy* 12:82–88.

Hannum, J. W. (1980). Some cotherapy techniques with families. *Family Process* 19(2):161–168.

Heilfron, M. (1969). Cotherapy: the relationship between therapists. *International Journal of Group Psychotherapy* 19(3):366–381.

Holt, M., and Greiver, D. (1976). Cotherapy in the treatment of families. In *Family Therapy*, ed. P. J. Guerin, pp. 417–431. New York: Gardner.

MacLennan, B. (1965). Cotherapy. *International Journal of Group Psychotherapy* 15:154–165.

McGee, T. F., and Schuman, B. N. (1970). The nature of the cotherapy relationship. *International Journal of Group Psychotherapy* 20:25–47.

Napier, A., and Whitaker, C. (1973). A conversation about cotherapy. In *The Book of Family Therapy*, ed. A. Ferber, M. Mendelsohn, and A. Napier, pp. 480–506. Boston: Houghton Mifflin.

_____ (1978). *The Family Crucible*. New York: Harper and Row.

Rabin, H. M. (1967). How does cotherapy compare with regular group therapy? *American Journal of Psychotherapy* 21:244–255.

Whitaker, C. A. (1977). Process techniques of family therapy. *Interaction* 1:4–19.

3

Cotherapy with a Borderline Patient

SEYMOUR HOFFMAN AND NILI KUPERMAN

In the extensive literature describing the borderline personality disorder, the classical symptomatology includes (1) poor differentiation of the self from objects, manifested by extreme vacillation between dependent overinvolvement with and withdrawal from significant others; (2) extreme narcissism; (3) pervasive splitting defenses manifested by sudden reversals in feelings about the self and others, and extreme vacillation between contradictory self-concepts (Kernberg 1977); (4) stable instability (Grinker et al. 1968) of mood and ego functions (e.g., impulsivity, acting out sexually and through drugs and periodical suicidal gestures with no clearly psychotic processes); and (5) confusion over sexuality and gender identity. Transient psychotic and depersonalization experiences are also not uncommon. The borderline patient is intolerant of normal levels of uncertainty and his thinking tends to be dichotomous.

In regard to treatment, the borderline's responses are often polarized as they alternate between magical and completely negative expectations. The therapist is often seen by the borderline patient as an object who will protect him against the outside world. He views the therapist alternately as all-powerful and completely worthless, and he does not experience concern or affection for him, but shifts from total dependence to total deprecation. Spatially, the borderline patient often needs physical distance between the therapist and himself in order to maintain a sense of his own integrity and avoid ego disintegration (Roller and Nelson 1991).

There exists little in the professional literature in the way of anecdotal description of treatment techniques to guide the psychotherapist in treating borderline patients (Reid 1989), as such treatment may still be considered "therapeutic heroics" (Silver 1983). Since the diagnosis of borderline personality disorder has been limited primarily to clients being treated by psychoanalytic therapists, the underlying assumptions are (1) that therapy takes a long time, (2) that clients' difficulties originated in early experiences that must be uncovered, and (3) that a major focus of therapy is the relationship with the therapist (Millman et al. 1982). The following is a description of the treatment of a patient with a severe borderline personality disturbance by cotherapists who used an unconventional, eclectic-strategic (Held 1984) therapeutic approach.

Case Study

> Vera, a 35-year-old single Jewish woman, applied to the clinic after she terminated treatment with a private psychiatrist. The treatment that she received during the three years included individual psychotherapy on a weekly basis and psychopharmacology. Treatment was terminated when the patient refused to participate in a day-hospital program or start looking for work, as recommended by the therapist. The clinical impression of the psychiatrist was that of a woman with a severe borderline personality disorder, with narcissistic and obsessive-compulsive features. Psychological testing, which was done at the request of the psychiatrist, presented a picture of a woman with a schizophrenic personality.
>
> Vera, for all purposes, lives with her parents even though they have provided her with a large furnished house next to theirs. At night, Vera retires to her own house to sleep. Vera's parents are well-to-do middle-class people who pampered her greatly when she was a child. They described her as being stubborn, difficult, and demanding. Vera views her parents as cold people who did not display any warmth or feeling toward each other or toward her. Her father is seen as a strong and

violent man, while her mother is viewed as kind and weak. Vera has strong ambivalent feelings toward them; on the one hand, she harbors deep anger and resentment toward them, and on the other hand, is very dependent and attached to them. Vera has little contact with her older brother and sister. All her life the patient felt that she lived in the latter's shadow, in that her sister was prettier, smarter, and more successful than she was.

After completing her army service, Vera worked for five years and functioned well. This period she described as being "the best years of my life." Things started to go downhill for Vera when at the prompting of her boyfriend, she began experimenting with hashish and cocaine. For a period of time, Vera went through extreme periods of confusion, as she experienced loss of identity and boundaries, felt she was going through a process of metamorphosis (that she was black, hairy, etc.), and was overwhelmed by feelings of emptiness and depression.

For the last several years, Vera's functioning has been severely restricted and hampered by strong obsessional ideas and compulsive rituals related to fears of contamination from people and her environment. She has not been able to work, has severed contact with her friends, and is presently being looked after by her parents.

After reading the psychiatric and psychological reports and interviewing the patient, the therapists (a male clinical psychologist and female psychiatric social worker) decided to treat Vera together for the following reasons and considerations:

1. Previously Vera underwent several years of unsuccessful dynamic psychotherapy, which resulted in her developing a strong erotic transference and dependency on the therapist, as she "lived from session to session." The presence of two therapists enables the dilution of these phenomena.
2. Since the ability to fuse good and bad images is frequently beyond the borderline patient's capacity, the presence of two therapists enables the patient to "split" ambivalent feelings toward them. The patient can select

one therapist to represent the reality principle and relate to him with relative consistency, and perceive him with minimal distortions, while being free to give fantasy reactions free rein and work through dramatic and irrational transference reactions to the other therapist (Mintz 1963).

3. Two therapists, by taking opposing views and roles in regard to the patient and his thoughts, feelings, behavior, and pathology, facilitate and promote externalization of his internal conflicts and ambivalent feelings and therefore make them available for therapeutic work and resolution. Also one therapist can provide support and emotional nurturance, while the other can reflect reality and consistently demand of the patient responsible and appropriate behavior (Hoffman et al. 1987, Chapter 1, this volume).
4. The presence of a male–female cotherapy team facilitates working through self and sexual identity conflicts, heterosexual relationship difficulties, and unresolved child–parent problems and issues.
5. Two therapists, by sharing the very difficult and demanding task of treating a borderline patient (with severe fluctuating pathology, provocative behavior, and suicidal threats and gestures) are emotionally more able to contain their own anxieties and frustrations and therefore are freer to focus on and attend to the patient's needs and pathology.

Treatment

The patient, a tall, slim, attractive woman who appeared younger than her stated age, entered the office in a rather dramatic and commanding manner. She selected a chair furthest from the therapists and sat throughout the session in a formal and rigid fashion. She gave evidence of her dirt phobia by minimizing her physical contact with her surroundings and by avoiding touching objects that she placed on or that fell to the floor. Vera was dressed and groomed in a highly provocative and eccentric fashion, and it was obvious that much time, effort, and forethought was devoted to her appearance. The patient spoke in a spontaneous and articulate manner and though her verbalizations reflected high intelligence, her behavior and demeanor frequently were commensurate with that of a young girl.

Vera placed all the responsibility of attending the clinic on her father and had doubts about needing treatment. She expressed ambivalent feelings about her former therapist; on the one hand, she had great respect and admiration for him, and on the other hand, she blamed him for her dependency and her isolation from the real world. Vera reported that she devotes most of her day to cleaning and organizing her house in a highly compulsive and ritualistic manner. She eats all her meals at her parents' house as she does not know how to cook and also because she does not like a mess in her house. Vera stated that she was willing to work but only if it was on the same level as her previous job.

At the cotherapist's suggestion, the next meeting was attended by the patient and her parents. The latter shared with the therapists their anguish and frustration in attempting to cope with their daughter's unpredictable and bizarre behavior, suicidal threats and gestures, and unrealistic demands. The father mentioned that in reference to employment, he had arranged that Vera would start working part time the following week as an assistant to a clerk in a small business. The psychologist (S. H.) at this point shared with the parents his reservations regarding the wisdom of this step, since in his view this would force the patient to accept and adapt to reality and set aside her fantasies and dreams, something that she had resisted doing for several years. He expressed his concern that as a result, her depression might deepen, and expressed caution in not moving too fast. The social worker (N. K.) challenged her colleague's pessimistic view and argued that by starting to work, Vera would begin the process of rehabilitation and she expressed confidence in the latter's motivation, strength, and persistence.

The patient returned the following week despondent and distressed. She felt humiliated doing simple routine work and said it was as though they "let all the air out of my balloon." She spoke of committing suicide by swallowing poison or jumping to her death. S. H. turned to his colleague and remarked that this was the reaction that he anticipated and feared. N. K. countered that Vera's frustration, anger, and despondency were the expected reactions of a person in the initial stages of the process of rehabilitation (reframing). She then described to Vera a movie she had seen about a famous athlete who at the peak of his career, was restricted to a wheelchair as a result of a serious car accident. The movie portrayed the athlete's anger, pain, fear, frustrations, and despondency as he began the process of rehabilitation. He succeeded, the social worker emphasized, because of his strong motivation and willingness to compromise, and within a year, he got around with crutches and became the team's head coach. Vera displayed keen interest in the cotherapist's conversation and said that the sessions were important to her.

In the following several sessions, Vera continued to complain about her work situation, social isolation, and compulsive behavior and rituals that were demanding a great amount of her time (hand washing, counting, etc.). She felt hopeless, depressed and saw no reason to continue living. The therapists continued in a provocative and supportive manner to present her with reality, in order to discourage and combat her strong regressive tendencies.

The next meeting was attended by Vera and her father at the latter's request and the former's acquiescence. The father expressed concern about his daughter's frequent suicidal threats and gestures and related that in the past two weeks, Vera had made several suicidal attempts. The therapist strongly advised the father to take this behavior seriously, and if it should occur again, immediately hospitalize his daughter in a psychiatric hospital. It is of interest to note that since that meeting, Vera has not threatened or made suicidal gestures.

In their regular presession consultation, the therapists decided to focus on the patient's distancing and avoidance behavior, which rendered her almost totally isolated from people. At the beginning of the session, S. H. stated that he understood

Vera's preference to sit far away from the therapists, as reflecting her fear of closeness and involvement with people. Vera responded in half-jest that if she sat any closer, one could touch and start up with her. N. K. inquired whether she does not trust the therapist or herself. When the patient failed to respond, S. H. invited Vera to experiment and sit closer to the therapists, and after some hesitancy and discomfort, she acceded to his request. The patient then recalled that after her previous therapist shook her hand, she became preoccupied with sexual thoughts and fantasies about him. N. K. observed that by distancing herself from people, Vera attempted to avoid uncomfortable and anxiety-producing thoughts, feelings, and experiences. The latter nodded her head in agreement.

The therapists also attempted on several occasions to deal with the patient's obsessive-compulsive behavior and rituals and dirt phobia through modeling (e.g., S. H. at times touched his shoes and the carpet and then his face and his co-worker's hand during the session) and task assignments (S. H. requested the patient to avoid washing her hands for two hours after touching the carpet in the office) but with little success. However, the patient did report that after the exercise for the first time in years she was able to touch her mother and even give her a back massage.

In the eighth meeting, Vera informed the therapists that her father had arranged an appointment for her in two weeks' time with a psychiatrist who was a well-known expert on treating compulsive behavior. She had great expectations from him as he was a professor and had an international reputation. After consulting our staff psychiatrist, who was treating her medically, the therapists informed the patient that they would send the requested information about her to the professor. They explained to her that they saw their task as helping her with her fears and difficulties in getting close and relating to people, and the psychiatrist's task as ridding her of her compulsive behavior.

In the course of conversation the following week, Vera mentioned that she does not allow people to ride in her car, including her parents. S. H. expressed curiosity regarding the patient's car and speculated that it was probably a very special and unique car, like its owner. Vera insisted that it was not and agreed to show it to the therapist, after he expressed an interest in seeing it. After admitting that truly it was nothing unusual, S. H. suggested that they all go for a short spin in it. After initially resisting, Vera drove the therapists around the block. The therapists thanked the patient for the ride and scheduled a meeting for the following week.

In the following meeting, N. K. asked the patient whether she had done an overhaul of the car after the last session. Vera responded that she had only cleaned the carpet where the former had sat. Vera then explained that entering her car is like entering her house, her privacy, herself, and she has not permitted anyone to enter any of the above in the last few years. At this point, S. H. speculated about what kind of a house the patient had and expressed an interest in seeing it. Vera refused and stated that even her parents are not allowed in except when something has to be fixed. S. H. remarked to his colleague that he was reminded of the high priest of Israel who was a very special and important person and only he alone was permitted to enter the holy of holies. However, he added, that if something had to be repaired, even a stranger or unclean person was permitted to enter the holy of holies. N. K. expressed her view that since the therapists' task was to help repair damage and malfunctioning, they were entitled to enter Vera's house. Again, after considerable resistance, Vera acceded, but insisted on a "very brief tour."

Before entering the large, attractive private house, at Vera's request, the therapists removed their shoes. The house, which was tastefully furnished and immaculately clean, had a museum-like quality to it: a place to visit but not to live in. The kitchen cupboards were bare and the windows and blinds were closed.

In discussing their visit in the next session, the therapists told Vera that they were now able to better understand and empathize with her depressed feelings. The sharp contrast and gap between the potential to live a comfortable and happy life and her monastic existence made a strong impression on them.

Vera nodded her head and said, "I reside there but I don't live there." N. K. encouraged Vera to let life into her beautiful house by opening the blinds and windows and inviting people inside. She suggested that possibly one of the sessions could be held in her house in the near future. Vera said she would consider it.

In the following session, Vera placed her chair near the therapists and remarked that she really sat too far away. She reported that she had met her new psychiatrist and was very much impressed with him, even though he had spent only twenty minutes with her and the medication was causing terrible side effects. S. H. suggested that the next meeting be held at the patient's house and requested Vera to prepare only coffee for them. Again after considerable hesitation Vera agreed.

Vera called on the morning of the scheduled meeting to inform the therapists that she was not feeling well because of the side effects of the medication, and that she had stopped working and stopped taking the pills because of this. Another meeting was scheduled for the following week.

On this visit the therapists entered the patient's house without being asked to remove their shoes. They noticed, in contrast to their first visit, that the windows and blinds were partially open. The therapists were served coffee, but when S. H. proceeded to open a box of cookies that he had brought along, the patient protested because of her concern that the crumbs would be dispersed on the table and floor. Vera pointed out that the therapists were the first people to sit on the living room chairs, as it was the first time she had hosted people. At the end of the visit session, Vera in half-jest asked, "Would you be willing to live here with me?" (reparenting). The therapists smiled, complimented her on being a good hostess, shook her hand, and departed.

In the following sessions, Vera continued to sit near the therapists and demonstrated more mature, genuine, and appropriate behavior and a more positive attitude and affect. She related in one session that the other day she had been able to touch several things in her parents' house and that she planned to meet a male friend of hers for coffee in town the following day. She also was considering inviting him to her house in the near future.

In the next meeting, the cotherapists decided to focus on the patient's unusual and eccentric mode of dress, which they saw as attracting considerable attention on the one hand, and on the other hand, distancing people. After the topic was raised, Vera explained that as a child she was unattractive, wore her older sister's used clothing and received little attention from people, and that was why it was important for her to dress in a unique manner. The decorative, heavy stockings that she wore even in the hottest weather, she explained, were to hide the excessive hair on her legs. She was very sensitive and distressed about her excessive hair and saw this as the reason why she avoided intimate contact with men. N. K. initiated a rather long "women's" discussion with Vera about the problem of hairiness for women. She related how she and her daughter deal with the problem by periodically shaving their legs, so that they could feel comfortable displaying them in public (normalization). S. H. at this point suggested that his colleague examine Vera's bare legs in his absence. Upon his return to the room, N. K. remarked to her co-worker that in her view Vera exaggerated the hairiness of her legs, and that by shaving them periodically she could readily remedy the problem. She added that it was unfortunate that she chose to hide such lovely legs behind thick stockings. At this point S. H. suggested that at the next meeting Vera appear stockingless, so that he could also view her legs. Vera smiled bashfully and said, "For you I'll do it."

In the following meeting, Vera appeared in an attractive blouse, short skirt, and bare legs. Proudly she displayed her nicely formed, clean-shaven legs and received compliments from the therapists on her appearance and on the significant step she had taken.

The therapists viewed Vera's latest behavior as a further step in allowing the removal of the protective walls and barriers that she had erected around herself. Previously she had permitted (with the aid of pressure and persuasion) the therapists to enter her car, then her house, then she opened the latter's windows and blinds, then she decreased the distance between herself and the therapists in the office, and the most recent move was to "expose" herself by removing her "protective" stockings.

Vera appeared radiant and full of confidence in this meeting. She reported that the side effects of the medication had subsided and that she had started to work at a different job that her father had arranged, which was more interesting than her previous job. She felt good at work and had a more positive attitude toward herself and toward life. She described herself poetically as a "wilted flower that came back to life and was beginning to grow." For the first time she saw the light at the end of the tunnel. Presently she views things differently, not in extremes but in various shades. She now realizes that her parents are not perfect but not as bad as she had thought in the past, and she was interested in improving her relationship with them.

Vera stated that she thought she could not get closer to people because of her hairiness. She mentioned that the experiment several weeks ago of sitting close to the therapists had helped her become aware of the distance between herself and others and today, in spite of her fears, she wishes to get close to people.

Several times during the session, Vera reassured the therapists that she wasn't "euphoric," that she had both her feet on the ground and that she had strong motivation to realize her maximum potential. At the end of the session, Vera looked at the social worker and said, "You believed in me and in my strengths." She then turned toward the psychologist and stated, "You didn't believe in me." The psychologist apologized for his insensitivity, poor judgment, and lack of faith and stated that he was happily surprised at the turn of events. He asked Vera how she explained the remarkable change and progress that had occurred in a rather brief period of time. Vera responded that she thought it was due to the medication. At this point both therapists vociferously challenged the patient's statement and argued that it was her strengths, motivation, and willingness to make changes and take risks and work on her problems and fears that produced the positive results. To reinforce their contention, they pointed out that the patient had started to make positive changes and progress before the pharmacological treatment was initiated.

It was important from the therapists' perspective to counter the patient's dependency, fatalism, and tendency to attribute success and failure to outside forces (parents, pills, etc.) and forcefully communicate the message to Vera that she alone was responsible for her behavior and fate. At their regular postsession discussion, the therapists decided to schedule a family session, in order for them to be able to appraise how her parents were reacting to the changes in their daughter and whether there was a need for their intervention into the family dynamics.

In the family meeting, Vera's mother expressed deep satisfaction regarding the positive changes and progress of her daughter. However, she complained about her daughter's continuing dependency on her and how this interfered with her daily life. The therapists pointed out how the parents were reinforcing this unwelcome behavior and made certain suggestions on how to modify the situation.

In the following meeting, Vera raised the issue of termination. The patient argued that she was confident in her ability to continue to progress at her own pace on her own and also that the individual sessions would interfere with potential employment. After discussing this issue from various aspects, the therapists suggested reducing the meetings to twice a month while, concomitantly, Vera would join an open group that the therapists were organizing at a more convenient hour. In the twenty-second session, Vera again raised the issue of terminating the individual sessions. In view of the patient's continuing progress and active participation in the group therapy meetings, the therapists acceded to her request. Several weeks later, Vera stopped attending the group meetings.

In an individual follow-up meeting initiated by the therapists, a year later, Vera reported that things were going well, her relationship with her parents was good, her obsessive-compulsive behavior was under control, and in the previous week she had hosted a male friend in her house and was extending her social contacts. Vera expressed interest in returning to therapy in the near future, in order to work on her dependency problems.

References

Grinker, R. R. Sr., Werble, B., and Drye, R. C. (1968). *The Borderline Syndrome.* New York: Basic Books.

Held, B. S. (1984). Toward a strategic eclecticism: a proposal. *Psychotherapy* 21:232–241.

Hoffman, S., Kohener, R., and Shapira, M. (1987). Two on one: dialectical psychotherapy. *Psychotherapy* 24:212–216.

Kernberg, O. F. (1977). The structural diagnosis of borderline personality disorganization. *Borderline Personality Disorders: The Concept, the Syndrome, the Patient,* ed. P. Hartocollis, pp. 87–121. New York: International Universities Press.

Millman, H. L., Huber, J. T., and Diggins, D. R. (1982). *Therapies for Adults.* San Francisco: Jossey-Bass.

Mintz, E. E. (1963). Special values of cotherapists in group psychotherapy. *International Journal of Group Psychotherapy* 13:127–132.

Reid, W. H. (1989). *The Treatment of Psychiatric Disorders.* New York: Brunner/Maze.

Roller, B., and Nelson, V. (1991). *The Art of Cotherapy.* New York: Guilford.

Silver, D. (1983). Psychotherapy of the characterologically difficult patient. *Canadian Journal of Psychiatry* 28:513–521.

4

Cotherapy with a Bulimarexic Patient

SEYMOUR HOFFMAN AND AVSHALOM MERDLER

The subclass of eating disorders that includes anorexia nervosa and bulimia is characterized by gross disturbances in eating behavior. Patients suffering from the above disorders seem to completely lack normal control, the former going far below their "set points" and even to the point of death, and the latter going beyond all the limits of any ordinary hunger (Pope and Hudson 1984). The essential features of anorexia nervosa are intense fear of becoming obese, disturbance of body image, significant weight loss (25 percent of original body weight), refusal or inability to maintain a minimal normal body weight, and amenorrhea in females (*DSM-III*).

The essential features of bulimia are episodic binge eating often of a high caloric content followed by depressed mood and self-deprecating thoughts. Bulimics often exhibit great concern about their weight and make repeated attempts to control it by dieting, vomiting, or using cathartics or diuretics. A large subgroup of anorexics alternate between starving and gorging. Boskind-Lodahl (1976) coined the term *bulimarexia* to describe these binge-starvers.

Various therapeutic approaches have been used in treating these eating disorders, with varying degrees of success. They include psychopharmacological (Pope and Hudson 1982), psychodynamic (Sours 1974), family therapy (Minuchin et al. 1978), behavioral (Stunkard 1972), group (Polivy 1981), and environmental controls via hospitalization (Crisp 1965). In this chapter, the treatment of a bulimarexic patient is described, using an active interactional cotherapy approach (Hoffman et al. 1987). In this approach, two therapists simultaneously treat the same patient, taking consistently *opposing roles* and views of the patient.

The Case of Leah

Leah, a 19-year-old woman who emigrated from Australia to Israel with her parents 18 years ago, appeared very thin, pale, and pathetic at the initial session. She was dressed in a modest fashion reflecting her religious background.

Leah related that her extreme diet began six months ago, and within four months her weight went from 125 to 99 pounds. She is five feet four inches tall. Her diet consists of one fruit every day during the school week. However, when she returns home for the weekend, she binges, which causes her to hate herself and become depressed. She revealed that at age 14, she went on an extreme diet and was seen for a short period of time by a psychiatrist at a hospital clinic following two suicidal attempts within a two-month period (ingestion of pills).

Leah's parents divorced when she was 2 years old. Her mother remarried six years later and at present Leah has six siblings. She remembers that as a youngster, she was obligated to function as a mother to her siblings. Her mother and stepfather fought frequently and because of this and the constant nagging by her stepfather to eat Leah decided to move in with her father who had also remarried. The patient was a very serious and highly motivated student and did well in school but poorly in the social area. She had few friends and was socially isolated. One and a half years ago, she started dating a boy, who is her stepfather's brother. He insisted that she seek assistance for her problems, and threatened to leave her if she refused treatment. After the intake, Leah was referred for a psychiatric evaluation. The psychiatrist recommended hospitalization in view of her suicidal ideation and anorexia. However, she refused to go along with the recommendation but agreed to outpatient treatment at the university's counseling service. After clinical evaluation of the situation and consultation with colleagues, it was decided that Leah would immediately be seen at the clinic, in view of her continuing deteriorating physical condition (i.e., her physical weakness, loss of hair, and amenorrhea).

Rationale for the Dialectical Approach

In light of the patient's poor motivation for treatment, past failures in therapy, ego-syntonic behavior, passivity, tendency toward dichotomous thinking, marked ambivalent feelings, fear of developing close personal relationships and exposing herself, primary use of denial and splitting as defense mechanisms, and the urgent need to change the patient's eating habits quickly, an active interactional cotherapy approach was used (Held 1984). This approach is especially effective with passive, resistant patients with limited insight and motivation for psychotherapy (Laub and Hoffman 1987, Chapter 11, this volume). In this approach the cotherapists can quickly and effectively challenge and confront the patient's maladaptive behavior, while at the same time provide support and encouragement for her so that she doesn't flee treatment (Hoffman and Laub 1986, Chapter 10, this volume).

Roles and Functions of the Two Therapists

Since the ability to fuse good and bad images is frequently beyond the anorectic's capacity (Solomon and Morrison 1972), it is anxiety relieving when this task can be avoided or postponed by projecting strong ambivalent feelings onto different persons. By virtue of the presence of two therapists, one supportive and one provocative, the patient could more readily understand her *contrary* feelings and express them without disrupting the relationship and therapeutic alliance.

In the first session, the patient spoke of her preoccupation with gaining weight. She saw herself as fat and desired to lose several more pounds so that she could see her bones. She stated also that her chest and thighs were too large. During the school week she maintains an extreme diet and avoids snack bars on the campus for fear that once she starts eating she won't stop. She is also careful not to carry any sweets in her bag for fear that she may give in to temptation. However, on weekends she throws caution and fear to the wind and binges.

At this point therapist P (provocative) left the room and returned a few moments later with his brunch. He explained that he had an ulcer and was required to eat at specific intervals. He offered some food and drink to the patient and his colleague. The patient refused while his colleague took the cookie offered and returned half of it, explaining that he was on a diet. In the presence of the patient, the therapists shared their views with each other (Hoffman and Gafni 1984, Chapter 2, this volume), and concluded that the patient's problem was that of lack of self-control and they saw a direct relationship between her binging and starvation. Since she was deprived of food all week, she was preoccupied with thoughts of food all the time and broke down on weekends. Instead of the patient deciding the time to eat, time (i.e., the day of the week) decided for her. To break this vicious cycle, she had to return to regular eating habits. Therapist P then suggested to Leah that she eat half of the cookie offered to her to demonstrate her willingness to attempt to resolve the problem. However, the patient refused, stating that she couldn't eat in the presence of the therapists. The therapist then placed the cookie in her bag and challenged her to return next week with only half a cookie eaten. Therapist S (supportive) expressed confidence that Leah was capable of doing this and thereby clearly demonstrating her motivation and ability to begin coping with this problem.

At the next session, the patient returned with the uneaten half of the cookie and received praise from both therapists, though therapist P's praise was preceded by expressions of disbelief at her accomplishment. Toward the end of the session, therapist S requested the patient to make a list of all the food eaten during the week and weekend, to establish more definitely for the patient the relationship between starving and binging. During the following session, after going over the "eating list" with the patient, therapist S asked the patient to choose either Monday or Wednesday next week to eat regularly. Therapist P objected and stated that the request was premature and unreasonable in view of the patient's lack of self-control and fear of gaining weight. However, the patient acquiesced to the therapist's request.

When she returned the following week with a positive report, the therapists responded in their respective familiar fashions.

Involving the Family

In view of the ongoing conflicts between the patient and her family regarding her dieting, it was decided to hold a family meeting. At this meeting, in which the patient's parents and stepfather appeared, Leah was encouraged to express her feelings (mostly pent-up anger and frustration) toward the family members. With some hesitation and stammering, Leah stated that her stepfather acted like a tyrant in the house. These remarks shocked the stepfather but brought smiles to the faces of the other family members. At the conclusion of the meeting, the therapists emphasized the importance of encouraging Leah's further growth and independence and requested the family members to cease nagging the patient about her food intake, to which they agreed.

In a subsequent session, therapist P stated the view that Leah did not wish to grow up, to be a woman and cope with issues related to independence and sexuality. By dieting, she became less feminine (amenorrhea and diminution of secondary sex characteristics), received a great deal of attention, and because of her situation, was not able to devote her energies and thoughts to important age-related issues. Therapist S countered his partner and stated that though the patient wants to grow and take upon herself adult roles and responsibilities, at the present time she is unable to deal with stressful situations in any other way.

Patient Reveals Dark Secret

In the following session, Leah, with much hesitation and anxiety, shared with the therapists her dark secret, that she had never shared with anyone before. From the age of 12 to a year ago, her stepfather, in spite of her objections, used to fondle her and insisted that she massage his back. She dared not reveal this to her mother for fear that this would only further aggravate their unstable marriage. Therapist S stated that it was clear to him why the patient decided to lose weight; it was her way of being less feminine, grown-up, and attractive to her lecherous stepfather. Therapist P said that it seemed that her stepfather was a sexual deviant and was in need of psychological treatment. Leah stated that all along her stepfather had given her the feeling that she was wrong and bad for rejecting his wishes and behavior and that now she saw him in a different light.

Patient's Condition Improves

In the next session, the patient expressed a great deal of anger toward her stepfather, who "caused her to go on extreme diets." She also spoke of her difficulty in expressing anger and being self-assertive and independent, her lack of self-confidence, and her tendency to stammer in anxiety-provoking situations, and her difficulty in coping with her controlling stepfather. As the session ended, Leah mentioned that she broke her extreme diet, started eating regularly, stopped bingeing on weekends, and that she was unconcerned whether she gets fat or not. She was complimented on her decision by both therapists, though therapist P expressed doubt about her ability to maintain this behavior. Leah agreed with his doubt. However, therapist S expressed confidence in the patient's ability to continue this behavior and stated that now she appeared ready to deal with her "deep psychological problems." Leah continued to eat regularly and within a short period of time, she gained weight and her menstrual cycle reappeared.

In the following weeks, the patient raised various issues and problems that were related to self-assertive behavior (with her stepfather, boyfriend, roommate, etc.), independence (stepfather buying all her clothes, financial dependence on parents, moving back to live with parents, breaking her engagement with her boyfriend, etc.) and marriage, sex, and motherhood.

Continuing with this dialectical approach, the therapists confronted Leah with her conflicts and maladaptive coping, and through the use of role playing they provided the patient with the opportunity to expand her behavioral repertoire and develop more effective means of dealing with stress and people (e.g., the therapists role played confronting her boyfriend regarding getting engaged, her roommate regarding her demanding behavior, her stepfather regarding his inappropriate behavior, etc.).

Exploring Negative Transference

In one session, to aid Leah to become more effective in dealing with authority figures (especially the stepfather), therapist S encouraged the patient to explore her feelings toward his partner (Treppa 1971) who behaved, at times in a "critical and tyrannical manner," just like her stepfather. Gradually, with the support of therapist S, the patient was able to express anger toward therapist P and challenge his views and assertions.

Termination

In view of the fact that Leah continued to progress, was now eating regularly, was looking well, had ceased to stutter, her concentration and academic functioning had improved, and she was more independent, self-assertive, and confident in her interpersonal relationships, the issue of termination was raised. One of the therapists was scheduled to depart shortly from the service. Leah agreed that the last session would be in a month's time, to coincide with the start of the long summer recess.

At the twentieth and last session, the patient was asked how she felt about being treated by two therapists simultaneously. She responded that in the beginning it was difficult and confusing for her being exposed to opposing views regarding herself and her behavior. However, she gradually got used to it and benefited from these experiences as it enabled her to become more aware of her conflicts and mixed feelings and provided her with the opportunity to more readily evaluate various possibilities and to choose and act more judiciously.

Since the therapists sensed that the patient still evinced an anorectic attitude toward weight and were also uncertain about how she would fare when confronted with pressure by her boyfriend and family to get married, a follow-up meeting was scheduled in three month's time, at the start of the new academic year.

Conclusion

This approach accomplished several important goals in a brief period of time, first and foremost being the restoration of normal weight and eating habits. By representing and reflecting her conflicts, ambivalences, and "divided self" in a consistent manner, the therapists enabled the patient to more quickly become aware of significant dynamic issues and her maladaptive responses.

Through role playing, the therapists were able to demonstrate alternative ways of dealing with anxiety-producing situations and at the same time, make the patient more sensitive to her difficulties and vulnerabilities as well as those of the significant people in her life. By assigning tasks to be done inside and outside the therapeutic situation, the therapists prompted the patient to modify her behavior and experiment with new ways of dealing with stress and the people around her.

Throughout the treatment period the two therapists generally presented consistently opposing views and attitudes regarding the patient and her behavior. However, on several important points they were of one mind, thus increasing the credence and weight of their stated viewpoint. These points included the seriousness of the patient's symptomatic behavior, viewing the patient's anorectic behavior as evidence of lack of self-control and stemming from unresolved interpersonal problems and conflicts, and bestowing praise on the patient when she demonstrated positive changes in her behavior. By virtue of one therapist challenging and confronting the patient's maladaptive coping mechanisms and the second therapist providing support and encouraging change and growth, the patient was enabled to recognize her ambivalent feelings, conflicts and inappropriate perceptions and behavior, and modify them in a relatively short period of time.

References

American Psychiatric Association. (1980). *Diagnostic and Statistical Manual of Mental Disorders* 3rd ed. Washington, DC: American Psychiatric Association.

Boskind-Lodahl, M. (1976). Cinderella's stepsisters: a feminist perspective on anorexia nervosa and bulimia. *Signs: Journal of Women in Culture and Society* 2:342–356.

Crisp, A. H. (1965). Treatment regime for anorexia nervosa. *British Journal of Psychiatry* 112:505–512.

Held, B. S. (1984). Toward a strategic eclecticism. *Psychotherapy* 21:232–241.

Hoffman, S., and Gafni, S. (1984). Active interactional cotherapy. *International Journal of Family Therapy* 6:53–58.

Hoffman, S., and Laub, B. (1986). Paradoxical interaction using a polarization model of cotherapy in the treatment of elective mutism: a case study. *Contemporary Family Therapy* 8:136–143.

Hoffman, S., Kohener, R., & Shapira, M. (1987). Two on one: Dialectical psychotherapy. *Psychotherapy* 24:212–216.

Laub, B., and Hoffman, S. (1987). A multimodal psychotherapeutic approach to a case of "matricide." *Family Therapy* 14:35–42.

Minuchin, S., Rosman, B. L., and Baker, L. (1978). *Psychosomatic families: Anorexia nervosa in context.* Cambridge: Harvard University Press.

Polivy, J. (1981). Group therapy for anorexia nervosa. *Journal of Psychiatric Research and Evaluation* 3:379–383.

Pope, H. G., and Hudson, J. I. (1982). Treatment of bulimia with antidepressants. *Psychopharmacology* 78:167–179.

_____ (1984). *New hope for binge eaters.* New York: Harper and Row.

Solomon, A. P., and Morrison, D. A. R. (1972). Anorexia nervosa: dual transference therapy, *American Journal of Psychotherapy* 26:480–489.

Sours, J. A. (1974). The anorexia nervosa syndrome. *International Journal of Psycho-Analysis* 55:567–576.

Stunkard, A. (1972). New therapies for the eating disorders: behavior modification of obesity and anorexia nervosa. *Archives of General Psychiatry* 26:391–398.

Treppa, J. A. (1971). Multiple therapy: its growth and importance. *American Journal of Psychotherapy* 25:447–457.

5

Indirect Treatment of Traumatic Experiences: The Use of Thematic Apperception Test (TAT) Cards

SEYMOUR HOFFMAN AND NILI KUPERMAN

Presenting Problem

Lem, a 13-year-old boy, was referred to the clinic by Eran (Israel Emotional First Aid) after he sought help in the middle of the night because of severe distress and fear of losing control over his angry feelings.

Family Background and History

Lem's family consists of working parents, both in their late thirties, and an 11-year-old sister.

The parents described Lem as an excellent student, serious, withdrawn, socially isolated, and preoccupied with seeking justice and protecting weak children.

They revealed that seven years ago they were referred to the clinic by the school guidance counselor after a tragic event. While playing with his 4-year-old cousin, Lem, then 6 years old, found his grandfather's gun and asked his maternal grandmother to unload it. However, one bullet remained in the gun chamber and was accidentally discharged while Lem pointed it at his playmate's forehead. The cousin was rushed to the hospital where she died. Lem was told that the girl died of complications of a lung infection. The police psychologist, after investigating the incident, referred him to the school guidance counselor who, in turn, referred him to the clinic. According to the chart notes, several sessions were held with the family where the focus was on marital and family conflicts. The only reference to the tragic incident was a note that the therapist recommended that the parents reveal the truth to the child at the proper time.

In the initial interview, Lem complained that he was very nervous and tense because of his sister's provocative behavior. He also mentioned that he had no friends and did not get along with his peers, especially girls. He said he felt discriminated against at home and that the whole world was against him. He has difficulty sleeping at night, has frequently entertained suicidal thoughts, and views his peers as "cruel monsters." He feels the closest to his dog. "I can trust him with my secrets." When asked what was the worst thing he did in his life, he responded, "I cursed my parents when I was five or six when I got angry at my sister." At the therapist's suggestion a family session was scheduled for the following week.

In the family meeting, Lem complained that he did not receive as much attention from his parents as his sister and that the latter did not respect his authority as older brother. For example, she did not heed him when he objected that she walked barefoot in the house or when she sat in the stairway at night. He explained that an accident could happen to her and he would blame himself. He saw himself responsible for his sister's welfare since his parents were tired and could not be relied on. "I must take responsibility for my sister and watch over her and I won't yield on this matter."

The therapist, struck with the possible connection between the boy's preoccupation and overconcern with his sister's well-being and the traumatic incident of seven years ago, requested a meeting with the parents to further explore this area. They were informed that a female therapist would also participate in the session.

At this meeting, the therapists shared with the parents their feelings about the possible relationship of Lem's unusual behavior and emotional distress with the traumatic incident. The parents expressed skepticism and pointed out that they had observed their son's behavior closely since the incident and were not aware of anything unusual or out of order. In fact the topic had never been raised or discussed, adding that they had been told not to tell the truth to their son. However, toward the end of the session, they admitted that in fact, they had been advised to discuss the incident with their son and tell him the truth "at the proper time."

The parents related that their relationship with the dead girl's father was not good, but insisted that it was because he was a difficult person. To prove their point, they recalled an incident where the latter screamed and threw a cake at Lem at his bar mitzvah party for no reason. They stated that they and Lem were on good terms with the rest of the family. They claimed that they have not been blaming him for the girl's death and did not talk about it. Every year the whole family visits her grave on the anniversary of her death.

The therapists emphasized the delicacy and sensitivity of the situation and recommended a slow and cautious approach. Psychological testing and another interview with Lem were suggested to get a clearer picture of his personality makeup, strengths and weaknesses, and defensive structure; they also wanted to get more information regarding how much he actually knew or wanted to know about the incident. The father readily agreed and informed the therapists that if Lem had to be told the truth, he would take on that responsibility.

In the individual session, Lem gave the impression of being a highly mature, intelligent, and articulate boy who related in a serious, attentive, and cooperative manner. Throughout all sessions, Lem appeared tense, anxious, and nervous. He frequently fidgeted in his seat, played with his fingers, and measured all his words carefully before speaking. He said that he tried to control his anger and not respond to provocations but at times he felt he was going to crack up and lose control. At those times he punches the wall. He remembers always being a tense and nervous child and having difficulty falling asleep.

In the session, the therapists attempted to explore in an indirect manner what Lem actually knew about the tragic incident by asking him to draw a family tree so that they could better familiarize themselves with his family and background (Guerin and Pendagast 1976).

When he started to speak about his mother's side, Lem indicated that she had an older sister with three children. After he spoke of his paternal grandfather's death five years ago, the therapists inquired whether there were any other recent deaths in the family. Lem at that point mentioned that he recalled now that his aunt's oldest daughter had died but he did not know of what cause. When asked whether it was a result of a sickness or traffic accident, Lem said he thought it was the latter. He claimed that he did not remember his reaction to her death.

The test findings depicted the boy as a highly intelligent, anxious, and conflicted person who was overwhelmed by intense feelings and impulses and was concerned about losing control over them. There were indications of an ineffective defensive system, tendency toward magical thinking, poor interpersonal relationships, and preoccupation with morbid thoughts, tragedy, and guilt feelings.

In view of the boy's history, symptomatology, and test findings, an indirect therapeutic approach was decided upon. Instead of focusing on Lem, the attention would be directed toward the boy's fantasy productions based on TAT cards (Holt 1951). An attempt would be made to relate to painful and inadequately suppressed material, reflect the child's inner conflicts, ambivalencies, distorted perceptions, unacceptable impulses and feelings, and fears. At the same time, therapy would strive to provide him with an alternate and healthier way of perceiving and coping with reality, emotions, conflicts, and painful experiences.

Lem's TAT stories were rich in content and death, tragedy, injustice, guilt feelings, loss, and punishment emerged as the main themes. After reviewing the stories and paying special attention to the heroes' dynamics, conflicts, perceptions, coping mechanisms, and the endings of the stories, the therapists in consultation, created their own contrasting stories to the particular TAT cards. The psychologist (S. H.) emphasized in his stories the id and rigid superego aspects of the hero, his unacceptable forbidden thoughts, fantasies, impulses, and maladaptive coping mechanisms, while the social worker (N. K.) stressed the healthy aspects of the heroes' ego, reality-oriented solutions, good judgment, control over impulses, flexibility, and constructive handling of their conflicts.

Three consecutive sessions were devoted to the presentation and discussion of eight out of twelve of the TAT stories. After reading Lem's story, the therapists presented their TAT stories. Then the three storytellers had an open discussion to decide whose version seemed the most appropriate. In the interaction, significant material was introduced. At the end of each deliberation, the social worker's arguments generally prevailed over the psychologist's view.

The following is an illustration of the above:

> Card 8BM: An adolescent boy looks straight out of the picture. The barrel of a rifle is visible at one side. In the background one can discern the dim scene of a surgical operation, like a reverie.

Lem's Story (with Therapists' Questions Interspersed)

It appears that here is a boy who saw someone who died. He didn't actually die. Someone he knows was wounded by a bullet of a gun. Two men who don't look like doctors are attempting to remove the bullet. The man looks unconscious. He doesn't seem to be in pain. The boy can't look at this. He is very sad. "Who are they?" They could be brothers. It doesn't seem to me that he will die because the bullet didn't enter the heart. It seems to me that he will recover and live and return to a normal life. "Whose rifle is it?" The rifle from which a bullet was discharged by mistake belongs to the wounded man. Or it could belong to the other brother. "What is he feeling?" If he shot the bullet, I think that he has guilt feelings, thinks he won't forgive him forever, hopes that he will live. "How does the story end?" I think that his brother will comfort him. It doesn't seem that it happened on purpose. The younger brother will learn. He won't handle a rifle again. They'll return to normal life.

Psychologist's Story

I see a child who is very worried and troubled because his brother was wounded by a bullet from a gun that he played with. The gun belongs to his brother. He played with the gun without permission and by accident a bullet was discharged and wounded his brother. This looks like an operating room and doctors are operating on him in an attempt to save him. The boy is very tense and nervous and is wondering whether his brother will live or die and will he forgive him for his deed. (Social worker: "How does the story end?") The brother dies after a few days. The boy will be miserable all the time. He won't permit himself to enjoy life because of his overwhelming guilt feelings, in spite of the efforts of his family to convince him that it was an accident and there was no reason to blame himself.

Social Worker's Story

I see a child who is worried about his brother who was wounded by a bullet that was discharged when he played with a gun. This can happen with children. The gun belongs to the brother or father. An accident happened and they're trying to save the brother. The boy is in shock and he hopes they'll save him because the bullet didn't enter a vital area. When the doctors see that the situation is hopeless, they call the boy so that he may bid farewell and separate from his brother. The boy stands by his side and expresses grief, explains that it was an accident, that he feels guilty, is in shock. The brother is not conscious and it's not clear if he heard him or not. (Psychologist: "How does the story end?") The parents will arrive at the hospital, will find the child in a stupor. The parents are also stunned and confused in the beginning and don't know what to say and how to react. However, they soon recover and attempt to comfort and reassure the boy and explain to him how they see the situation and then he is able to express his feelings, pain, guilt and his longings for his brother and speak of the injustice that occurred to him and the desire to atone for his deed. The relatives of course continue to reassure him that it was an accident and though it may be difficult for him to understand it as a child, for children tend to view things in relation to consequences and not intentions, in time, after many discussions with the child, who seems serious and intelligent, he will gradually absorb and accept what the relatives explain to him and will forgive himself and will succeed to live a normal life.

At this point Lem was asked to talk about the different stories presented by the therapists.

Lem: I still think that the gun belongs to the boy and if he's 13 or 14, it is possible that he owns a gun if they rely on him.

Social Worker: Does the boy in the story forgive himself?

Lem: No. Even if his brother forgives him.

S.W.: How long will he feel guilty?

Lem: Five, ten years. He was still wounded and there will remain a scar or some disability. The boy will be preoccupied all the time with thoughts of what will happen and how he could have prevented it.

Psychologist: What do you think will enable him to forgive himself after five, ten years?

Lem: That he will see that his brother really forgave him.

P.: Do you think that after only five or ten years he will be able to forgive himself and live a normal life?

Lem: Not completely normal like in the past. In the future he will be more careful, if they give him a gun.

P.: He will be able to overcome this terrible experience?

Lem: Little by little he will forget this incident.

S.W.: But five, ten years is a long period of time especially for a child. So much time will have to pass before he will forgive himself, and especially since his brother and family forgave him and didn't blame him and understood that it was a freak accident?

Lem: Maybe not ten years, maybe five. He will be depressed for a period of time and won't handle guns anymore.

P.: If the boy is 13 then he is already past bar mitzvah (confirmation) and therefore he is responsible for his actions. I don't see how he can stop feeling guilty and responsible for his deed.

S.W.: Do you think one can hold a 13-year-old responsible for his behavior? He's only a child.

P.: According to the Jewish religion, a 13-year-old assumes responsibilities of a man. He is obligated to keep all the commandments. To underscore this, at his bar-mitzvah, the father of the boy recites a blessing freeing himself of responsibility for the child's actions from that moment on.

S.W.: But he's still a child even though he is obligated to keep the commandments. He is dependent, not fully mature, and not completely responsible for his actions in the eyes of religion and the law.

At this point the psychologist accepted his colleague's view and reinforced it by pointing out that according to the Bible one had to reach the age of 20 to be officially counted, serve in the army, and be deserving of punishment from heaven.

The social worker raised the issue of moral judgment and made the point that according to Piaget (1962) and other researchers, a child around the age of 6 tends to focus on and emphasize consequences of behavior and not intentions. As the child grows and matures cognitively, he begins to place more emphasis on intentions of behavior. Therefore, a 13-year-old boy would appreciate the fact that the tragedy was a result of an accident and would be able to forgive himself.

At this point she presented to Lem a moral judgment situation question to which he responded on a cognitive level appropriate to a mature boy.

After the three TAT story sessions, the therapists scheduled a meeting with the parents to obtain information regarding Lem's functioning and behavior during the last few weeks, and also to explore with them their readiness to discuss openly the past tragic incident with their son.

In the session, the parents reported that they did not see any significant change in Lem's behavior, but that he was enjoying the sessions.

The therapists shared with the parents their view of Lem, the psychological findings, and read several of his TAT stories. The parents reactions were highly emotional. Lem's mother was shocked to hear that her son was so distressed, guilt ridden, and preoccupied with death and tragedy. The father exclaimed that "the topic is alive with him, he knows everything but it seems that he wasn't able to discuss and work it out." The therapists encouraged the parents to accept the idea of raising the issue with Lem in a family therapy session and suggested how the topic could be raised and handled in a tactful, sensitive, and effective manner. After much deliberation, discussion, and soul-searching, the parents agreed and a family meeting was scheduled for the following week.

In the family session, the therapists mentioned that Lem was a very anxious boy who was very much preoccupied with issues and thoughts concerning death, tragedy, guilt, punishment, and injustice. This they felt was very unusual for a boy his age and inquired of the parents whether they could shed light on this matter. The father mentioned that Lem never permitted himself to be a child, to be happy and carefree, and instead tended to take upon himself too many responsibilities.

Lem chimed in that from grade one through six he identified and was part of the "out" group and suffered greatly from this. Similar to the ex-Vietnam veteran, he was still carrying the scars and the negative effects of the war, many years later. To the social worker's question whether he had experienced any serious tragedies or traumas in his life that could possibly explain his present morbid preoccupations and pessimistic outlook, Lem answered in the negative. The father at this point confronted his son and reminded him that not many years ago a tragedy did occur and pressed him to talk about it. Lem, with considerable discomfort, conceded this fact and related that some years ago, he accidentally shot his young cousin while playing with his grandfather's gun. At the therapists' urging and prompting, Lem described in detail the incident but wasn't sure about the final cause of his cousin's death. The rest of the family members were encouraged to participate in the discussion of this taboo topic. They did, though with considerable uneasiness. Lem's sister volunteered that she remembers being extremely shocked and upset upon discharge of the bullet. Lem stated that he does not remember his reaction then and opined that the incident didn't have any negative impact or influence on him then or later on.

The psychologist stated that he saw a definite relationship between the past tragic event and the boy's behavior, mood, and TAT stories. Upon receiving Lem's permission, he proceeded to read the boy's stories to card 16 and card 8BM, in order to support his contention.

Card 16 (Blank): Lem's Story (with Therapists' Questions Interspersed)

I imagine a noisy railroad station. It's a period of war. Many soldiers. A mother is waiting for her son. She is worried that the train's about to leave and her son has not appeared. Suddenly he alighted from the train, wounded and supported by two of his friends. He'll return home physically disabled and will not be able to return to the battlefield, and the mother will be happy. "What happened to him?" Maybe he was shot by the enemy or his vehicle ran over a mine. "What is he feeling?" Feels very bad. Ashamed that he was wounded. Thinks of his friends who are fighting and being killed. Feels he did something bad, that he wasn't alert and careful and was thereby wounded. "What bad thing did he do?" He wasn't observing orders or if he went over a mine, didn't pay attention to the road. "How does the story end?" He will forgive himself.

At this point, the social worker supported her colleague's assertion and with Lem's permission read the boy's story to card 13B, of a little boy is sitting on the doorstep of a log cabin.

Card 13B: Lem's Story (with Therapists' Questions Interspersed)

A house in the hills. A boy is playing a harmonica. His parents are poor. He appears sad, depressed, and without hope and his escape is to sit at the entrance of the house and play his harmonica. "Why is he sad?" It could be that his parents don't allow him to own an animal or that he had one but it died. Could be he had a dog or horse. "Why did the animal die?" Could be the animal died from a sickness or an accident. "How does he feel?" Feels guilty that he let him go by himself, that he didn't take care of him adequately. The animal fell or died of hunger. "How does the family feel?" The family doesn't blame him. He blames himself without reason. "How old is the boy?" He looks like he's 5 or 7 years old. "How does the story end?" In the future it appears that he will recover from this and get another pet, even of the same kind. He really longs for the dead animal and will name the new one after him. He will give to him more love than to the previous pet, as if it were the same animal that went and returned. He will watch over it more than before so nothing will happen. "How will he do this?" Feed it all the time, watch over it so it won't go any place.

The social worker then added, "And not go barefoot and not sit alone in the stairway at night."

Lem didn't accept the therapists' views and explained that the boy in the story in card 13B was the same boy as in the previous story (card 8BM). In response to the therapist's inquiry, the parents agreed that they saw a relationship between Lem's conflicts, behavior, TAT stories, and the tragic event. Lem's sister, however, supported Lem's contention that the same boy was the subject of the stories in cards 13B and 8BM.

At the therapists' suggestion, an individual meeting was scheduled with Lem for the following week.

In the next meeting, an attempt was made to assess the effect of the previous session. Lem, in his characteristic manner, downgraded the significance and import of the session and complained that his parents continued to treat him as a little child and limit his freedom.

In the session with the family two weeks later, the parents did not mention the past "dramatic" session and traumatic event. When questioned by the therapists, they mentioned that the family held an extensive and open discussion about the traumatic event and this had a positive and liberating effect upon the family members. They also reported that Lem displayed less concern regarding his sister's health and well-being. However, overall they expressed disappointment and anger that Lem's rebellious behavior and unwillingness to compromise and cooperate with them had shown so little improvement.

From this point on, the therapy sessions took on the form and characteristics of typical family therapy discussions with a focus on adolescent-parental conflicts.

Discussion

Prior to therapy, as a result of the gentleman's agreement between the family members and the boy that the tragic event would not be discussed, Lem never had the opportunity to work out the traumatic incident. The issues of responsibility, blame, guilt, and punishment remained confused and blurred over the years for the child. This confusion was compounded by the mixed messages sent by the family members. On the one hand, the manifest message was that he was blameless, on the other, the latent message was that he was guilty.

In view of the ineffectiveness of denial and suppression as evinced by Lem's symptomatic complaints, unusual behavior and emotional distress, an indirect therapeutic approach was used in order to avoid alerting and threatening his weak defensive system.

Using the TAT stories, painful and relevant issues were raised, suppressed material was brought to the fore, and intense ambivalent feelings and thoughts were reflected. The rigidity of Lem's perceptions and superego was unmasked and alternate, more flexible and constructive ways of viewing and coping with difficulties and conflicts were introduced.

As a result of this approach, the ground was slowly and carefully prepared for relating to and coping with the taboo topic in an open and direct manner. Once brought out into the open, Lem's distorted perceptions, maladaptive behavior and symptomatic complaints could be more readily comprehended and addressed in further therapy sessions.

The effectiveness of this approach in highly sensitive and delicate situations should be further explored. Its applicability with adults and younger children (using the CAT and HAT) where a cautious approach is warranted, would seem to be a worthwhile and interesting venture.

References

Guerin, P. J., and Pendagast, E. G. (1976). Evaluation of family system and genogram. In *Family Therapy*, ed. P. J. Guerin. New York: Gardner.

Hoffman, S., Kohener, R., and Shapira, M. (1987). Two on one: dialectical psychotherapy. *Psychotherapy* 24:212–216.

Holt, R. (1951). The thematic apperception test. In *An Introduction to Projective Techniques*, ed. R. Holt and G. L. Anderson. Englewood Cliffs, NJ: Prentice Hall.

Piaget, J. (1962). *The Moral Judgment of the Child.* New York: Collier.

6

Phantom Cotherapist

SEYMOUR HOFFMAN AND HEDVA SEGAL

The effectiveness of an active interactional cotherapy approach in dealing with difficult, resistant, and poorly motivated patients has been described in various articles (Hoffman and Laub 1986, Hoffman et al. 1987, Hoffman and Merdler 1988, Chapters 10, 1, and 4, this volume). In this chapter, a modification of this approach is described in the treatment of a highly resistant, suicidal Arab woman by a Jewish psychology intern.

Case Report

> Fatima, a 23-year-old single Arab woman presented herself for the second time to the university's psychological counseling service. She had been seen initially by a senior staff member but after several sessions terminated treatment. At this time, she requested a female therapist from a similar ethnic background (Arab), "someone who could understand her background, mentality and culture." She also emphasized that a male therapist could not help her.
>
> Throughout the session, Fatima chain-smoked, which according to her was exceptional for an Arab woman from a good family. The patient lives in a large village in Galilee, with two unemployed parents and twelve siblings, who are all married, except her two younger brothers.

In the first therapy session, Fatima related that she had made several suicidal attempts in the past (ingestion of pills, poisonous substances, and gas inhalation) and much to her chagrin, was unsuccessful. "Even to die, I don't have any luck in life."

The precipitating event that caused her deteriorating condition and depression was unrequited love. At the age of 16, she met a boy from her village who captured her heart. For four years they corresponded but never met alone as dictated by her tradition. On her twenty-first birthday, she was informed by the youth that he intended to marry another girl and a year later he did so.

Fatima became depressed, cried continually, refused to meet other men, lost 20 pounds, and experienced difficulty in sleeping without medication and in concentrating on her academic studies. She lost her trust in men, was disgusted with life, and had on many occasions attempted to cut it short.

The therapist attempted to make a contract with the patient regarding her suicidal behavior but with little success. Instead of contacting the therapist when she felt suicidal, the patient took an overdose of pills.

Because of the strong suicidal risk and steady deterioration of her functioning, a psychiatric evaluation was arranged. However, Fatima didn't keep the appointment because of her fear that she would be hospitalized and because the psychiatrist was a man. "I don't trust men, I don't want their help, and accepting help from them is demeaning."

In supervision, the therapist, a young psychology intern, shared with her supervisor her anxieties, fears, and frustrations in working with this woman and her difficulty in accepting total responsibility for the case. It was decided that she would suggest to the patient that a senior staff person would participate in the next meeting for purposes of evaluation. It was theorized that, in view of the patient's history, the presence of a male therapist from a Western cultural background may have a beneficial impact on the therapeutic stalemate. It was also decided that an active interactional cotherapy approach would be employed, in view of the impasse in therapy and the criticalness of the situation. The supervisor-consultant would confront and challenge the patient's maladaptive defenses and destructive behavior while the therapist would support the patient and thereby strengthen their tenuous relationship.

The therapist prepared the patient for the meeting, pointing out to her that though the consultant is an aggressive and opinionated man, he has a great deal of professional experience and she respects his clinical judgment.

At the joint meeting, the consultant, after being updated about the patient and the treatment, opined that the patient is a very immature, impulsive, and passive person who is seeking someone to solve her problems for her. When confronted with disappointment and frustration, like a little child, she attempted to solve her problems through suicide. The consultant expressed doubt that in view of her immaturity and past history of suicidal behavior, that she can be treated on an outpatient basis.

The therapist countered, that in spite of her difficulties and depression, Fatima had continued her university studies, had faithfully attended the therapy sessions, and that at times demonstrated mature behavior and good judgment.

The consultant ridiculed the therapist's optimistic assessment and suggested another meeting in a month's time for a reevaluation of the situation.

In the following meeting, Fatima related that the previous session was very difficult for her and that the consultant ruined her whole day. It angered her that every time the therapist supported her, he belittled her even more. She agreed to another meeting with him because "he belittled me so much that I have to prove to him that he's wrong. I'm not a little girl."

In the following supervisory session, the therapist requested that the supervisor continue as a cotherapist on a regular basis in view of the positive results. However, the latter stated that it was counterindicated in view of the patient's strong hostility toward him. Also, it appeared to him that the figure of the consultant is already "a salient factor as shadow member of a triadic relationship" (Bernard et al. 1980). By the therapist frequently referring to him in the sessions, his presence will be further strengthened. She would also be able to exploit his absence by attributing to him provocative and challenging views and, at the same time, not assuming responsibility for them and thereby protect the tenuous relationship between her and the patient.

In the next meeting, Fatima spoke about her revulsion regarding the traditional marriages where the woman is forced to deny and subjugate her identity to that of her husband and that her sole role is to produce and raise children. In spite of her respect for her tradition and religion, she wasn't willing to concede her independence and meet men and get married. The therapist responded that if the consultant was present, he would insist that this was just an excuse to avoid contact and relationships with men because of her lack of trust and fear of being hurt and disappointed again. She, on the other hand, could understand the difficulties, conflicts, and reservations of a woman from an Arab village who is in constant contact with a culture with Western values.

In the second joint meeting, the consultant, in spite of the therapist's positive report regarding the patient, expressed doubt that she was capable of maintaining this positive trend and predicted that when she will be confronted with a disappointment or difficulty at home or at school, she'll return to her old ways of coping, that is, suicidal behavior. The therapist protested and challenged the consultant's assessment and prognosis and pointed out that in the last several weeks the patient hadn't raised the topic of suicide, had gained weight, and was sleeping better. The patient was furious at the consultant and remarked sarcastically, "you think you know everything."

Two months later, on Fatima's birthday, in spite of the therapist's efforts to prepare the patient to deal with the anniversary of her former boyfriend's engagement to another woman, the patient swallowed a large amount of sleeping pills, in order not to be conscious that day.

The following day, she expressed feelings of despair and hopelessness and stated that if she didn't get out of the depressed situation within a month, she will kill herself. The therapist responded that it seems that the consultant was correct in his assessment and that maybe it was a mistake not to have hospitalized her. With the patient's acquiescence, a third joint meeting was scheduled.

At this meeting, the consultant chided Fatima for not being able to part emotionally from her former boyfriend, that she is continuing to mourn his loss, and as proof to his claim, he pointed out that she still carried his picture in her wallet. He also opined that the patient still harbors a great deal of anger and hostility toward her former love that she isn't willing to relinquish.

The therapist asked the consultant what steps Fatima could take to demonstrate her sincerity regarding her desire to part from her former love and look to the future. He responded that in his view, a meaningful act would be to remove her former boyfriend's picture from her wallet and burn it (Van Der Hart 1981), which he doubts that she is capable of doing. The therapist countered that she thought Fatima was capable of doing this.

Fatima denied vehemently all of the consultant's assertions and angrily declared that she wasn't willing to see him again.

In the following session Fatima related that she removed the picture from her wallet to prove the consultant wrong. The next few weeks were unremarkable until a conflict erupted between Fatima and her family. The patient again spoke of suicide, didn't go out of the house, and proclaimed that "people are hypocrites and one can't trust anyone."

Attempts by the therapist to confront the patient by "bringing in" the consultant were of little avail. Feeling dejected, frustrated, angry, and exasperated because of the patient's unpredictable vacillations between progress and relapse, and the frequent suicidal threats, the therapist begged to be relieved of the case.

In supervision, it was decided to exploit the therapist's feelings in an attempt to shake up the present therapeutic impasse.

In the next meeting, the therapist shared with Fatima her terrible feelings of disappointment, frustration, and anger and irritation at herself for having failed to help her get out of her morass. She should have accepted the consultant's advice and not have attempted to treat her on an outpatient basis. It seems that she overestimated the patient's strengths and motivation and her own ability and underestimated the consultant's knowledge and perceptiveness.

To strengthen the impact on the patient, the therapist related to her a nightmare she "had" the previous night. "I am sitting at the bottom of a mountain and standing on its top is the consultant. His face is stern and angry and he's pointing his long finger at me, shouting 'I told you so. I told you so. You are guilty and responsible for her death because you didn't listen to me. Her suicide will be on your conscience all your life."

"I started to cry and begged for forgiveness but it was to no avail. Then I woke up in a sweat."

Fatima was greatly affected by this "confrontation" and in an emotional manner apologized to the therapist for disappointing her.

In the following meeting, Fatima announced that she received a proposal from a man she knew from her village, who in the past expressed interest in her, and she agreed to see him secretly.

During the next few months, Fatima appeared to be functioning and coping more effectively, in spite of academic pressures and final exams. A month before graduation the issue of termination of treatment was raised. Fatima expressed the opinion that she had been helped greatly by the therapist, had faith and trust in her and in her opinions but was not interested in continuing therapy with another person in another setting. However, she agreed to a follow-up meeting in three months.

In the last session she stated that in the past year and a half, she felt she had matured six years. The therapist, in her view, understood and accepted her and her culture and mentality, something that the male therapist failed to do. In reference to the consultant, she opined that even though he attacked her, she was helped by him because it forced her to confront issues, feelings, and thoughts she tended to avoid and change her behavior.

Fatima reported that she was continuing to see her male suitor every day secretly to get to know him better, and that after graduation she planned to seek employment as a teacher.

Discussion

The direct involvement of the consultant as a cotherapist in the therapeutic proceedings, though quite limited (three out of thirty-three sessions) had an important effect and impact on both the therapeutic process and outcome and on the therapist.

In regard to the former, the consultant's interventions forced the patient out of her passivity and impelled her to deal with issues, dynamics, and conflicts that she characteristically avoided. Because of the tenuous relationship that existed between the therapist and the patient, the therapist dared not confront the patient directly. However, "through" the consultant, she was able to challenge the patient's ineffective defenses and maladaptive behavior throughout the period of therapy, in a forceful and effective way. As Peggy Papp (1983) pointed out, "Outrageous suggestions are often more effective coming from an unseen authority outside the session than from a trainee who is then called upon to defend them."

Also, the consultant (the prototype of the feared and hated male) by attacking and belittling the therapist (let alone the patient) forced the patient to come to the therapist's rescue by cooperating with her (Papp 1983).

In regard to the effect on the therapist herself, it is obvious that a difficult and frustrating case such as this one, with the constant threat of suicide dominating the picture and where the previous efforts of a senior therapist had failed, can be an overwhelming experience for any therapist, let alone a trainee, to take upon herself alone.

The limited direct involvement of the consultant in the therapy first and foremost diminished the anxiety and loneliness of responsibility that characterizes most clinical work. It also provided the therapist with a direct modeling and an *in vivo* experience of an experienced clinician at work. At the same time, the supervisor was able to achieve a better feeling for what the trainee was dealing with. Finally, it contributed to the therapist's professional development and growth as she was able to see the supervisor deal with particular situations without the benefit of hindsight, especially when supplemented by subsequent discussions about the rationale for particular interventions (Bernard et al. 1980).

It is interesting to note that in spite of the fact that the therapy took place during the Intifada (Arab uprising in the territories captured by Israel in 1967) and that the patient attended an Israeli university during the day and returned to her Arab village in the evening (which at times was under curfew), the issue of Arab-Israeli relations and, more specifically, its effect on the therapeutic relationship did not come up in the therapy in spite of the sensitive attempts by the therapist to explore these issues (Gorkin 1986).

One can hypothesize that because of the strong need of the patient to identify with and relate to another person (therapist) of the same sex and cultural background (especially after an unsuccessful experience with her previous therapist), the patient wasn't willing to take the risk of jeopardizing the relationship by alluding to these sensitive issues. In spite of this, significant therapeutic progress was made.

References

Bernard, H. S., Babineau, R., and Schwartz, A. J. (1980). Supervisor trainee cotherapy as a method for individual psychotherapy training. *Psychiatry* 43:138–145.

Gorkin, M. (1986). Countertransference in cross-cultural psychotherapy: the example of Jewish therapist and Arab patient. *Psychiatry* 49:69–79.

Hoffman, S., and Laub, B. (1986). Paradoxical interaction using a polarization model of cotherapy in the treatment of elective mutism: a case study. *Contemporary Family Therapy* 8:36–43.

Hoffman, S., Kohener, R., and Shapira, M. (1987). Two on one: dialectical psychotherapy. *Psychotherapy* 24:212–216.

Hoffman, S., and Merdler, A. (1988). Use of dialectical psychotherapy in treating bulimarexic disorders: a case study. *Journal of Contemporary Psychotherapy* 18:92–102.

Papp, P. (1983). *The Process of Change*. New York: Guilford.

Van Der Hart, O. (1981). Rites of separation in strategic psychotherapy. *Psychotherapy* 18:-188–194.

7

Cotherapy with an Iatrogenically Infantilized Patient

SEYMOUR HOFFMAN AND IRIS HOROWITZ

In the process of assessing patients with past histories of psychotherapeutic treatments, the interviewer should determine whether the patient is impaired to the extent that he is in need of continual treatment. There are patients whose psyches have been damaged by either trauma or severely inadequate parental care who cannot function without lifetime maintenance treatment. These patients fall into the category of "interminable" patients. "The complexity of emotionally reparenting a person, providing the missing dimensions of a scarred psyche, is a timeless process" (Travers 1986). Patients with such a past generally have histories of marginal functioning, previous hospitalizations, suicidal attempts, and decompensation when treatment has been terminated.

However, there are patients with relatively healthier egos who continually seek psychotherapeutic treatment despite their poor responses in the past to treatment, because treatment is a way of life for them. As a result of their tendency to present themselves and their past and present functioning in a one-sided, negative manner, and their insistence on receiving psychological help, their requests are too frequently honored. The result is the creation of an "iatrogenically infantilized" patient (Frances et al. 1984).

The following is a description of a nonconventional approach to a "professional" patient by cotherapists.

Case Study

Dan, a 24-year-old single college student, presented at the initial intake with a long list of complaints and problems. Among them were his fears of establishing relationships with people, especially those of the opposite sex, feelings of isolation, lack of self-confidence, conflicts with his parents, depression, mental paralysis, confusion, and general feelings of hopelessness and helplessness. The patient related information about himself in a spontaneous, compulsive, disorganized, and detached manner.

The intaker's impression was that of a highly anxious, tense, and dependent individual with many emotional and psychological conflicts, who was in need of long-term dynamic and supportive therapy.

Several weeks before his appointment with his assigned therapist (I. H.), Dan called her at home at 11 o'clock at night and shared with her his anxieties and problems. He requested an earlier appointment and also gave her the telephone number of his previous therapist in case she would like to receive more information.

The therapist decided to consult a staff member regarding the feasibility of accepting Dan at the student counseling service. In view of his abundant emotional conflicts and previous history of unsuccessful treatment experiences and strong dependency needs, it was questionable whether the student counseling service was the right facility, since the patient appeared to be in need of long-term treatment. An appointment was scheduled by the therapists to see the patient the following week.

Dan, a tall, well-built man with a serious and tense expression on his face, entered the interview room hesitantly. Throughout the session he spontaneously spilled forth his difficulties, fears, complexes, failures, and symptoms without making eye contact with the interviewers. The message so effectively communicated was that he was a "mental mess" and was in need of immediate long-term, intensive treatment.

Dan inquired whether he could be seen by a psychiatrist and whether he could be treated by medication or hypnosis. He stated that he required at least three years of treatment.

Dan volunteered that he had been in psychological treatment since age 13 with several therapists. Though he spent many hours discussing with them his unhappy childhood, poor relations with his parents and siblings, feelings of rejection and discrimination, fears, and his failure to establish relationships with his peers, little substantive improvement had occurred in his condition over the years. He criticized one therapist for exploiting him sexually and the others for not being sufficiently involved and sensitive to his difficulties and problems.

Throughout the meeting, Dan focused on his shortcomings. However, when asked about his three years' military service, the patient admitted that he completed it successfully even though he felt estranged from his peers and frequently was the target of exploitation and ridicule. Academically he was doing well, in spite of having difficulty in concentrating.

Dan revealed that he was the third of four children. He described all his siblings as successful in their academic, professional, and social endeavors. His father, a Holocaust survivor, was described as weak and apathetic, while his mother was described as strong and domineering. He was the "good" child in the family who always tried to please his parents and therefore was punished less than his siblings.

Toward the end of the interview, the therapists informed Dan of their strong reservations about accepting him for treatment at the counseling service. They pointed out to him that the clinic worked primarily with students with more strengths who could benefit from short-term therapy. In view of his past history, present situation, and insistence on long-term treatment, they had doubts about his suitability. The patient was instructed to return home and explore whether he had sufficient strengths and motivation to benefit from this kind of therapy, and to return the following week with his response (O'Connell 1984).

Treatment

The therapists, after considerable deliberation, decided upon a brief program in which the focus would be on the adult part of the patient's life, on the here and now,and the future.

Emphasis would be placed on actions and behavioral changes. Catharsis and past events with emphasis on obtaining overall insight were not primary goals. Instead of joining the patient in the basement (past, inner life), the therapists would insist that he join them on the ground floor (present, reality). In this fashion they hoped to discourage the fostering of dependency and regression and the iatrogenic infantilizing process.

To further decrease Dan's feeling of inferiority, helplessness, and dependency, and deemphasize the patient–therapist relationship, the therapists decided to informalize the meetings by inviting Dan to join them for coffee during the sessions.

A cotherapy approach (Hoffman et al. 1987, Chapter 1, this volume), was decided upon so that the patient's maladaptive defenses and strong regressive needs could be more directly and effectively challenged, while at the same time, provide him with sufficient encouragement and support to enable him to continue in therapy and direct his energies toward change and growth.

In view of the absence of a strong, supportive male figure in Dan's life, it was decided that the male therapist (S. H.) would assume the positive, encouraging role, while the negative, challenging role would be assigned to the female colleague (I. H.).

The goals of therapy were to increase and improve Dan's self-image and confidence, autonomous functioning, independent thinking, and enable him in the shortest time possible to pursue his life without therapy.

In the second meeting, as expected, Dan grudgingly agreed to the conditions set down by the therapists. Therapy would be for a period of nine months with two therapists. Toward the end of the session, S. H. suggested that the patient, in view of the limited time available for treatment, participate also in a group conducted by the therapists, to aid him in overcoming his difficulties in relating to his peers. I. H., however, expressed reservations about Dan's ability to effectively cope in a group at this time, in view of his fears and limited experience. She also expressed the opinion that this "premature" move might exacerbate the patient's psychological problems and also impede the work of the group. In spite of Dan's objections, S. H. insisted, pointing out that it would be a valuable experience for him and that he was confident that the patient would effectively cope with the situation.

The third session took place after Dan's first group-therapy experience. He received considerable positive feedback from the therapists regarding his performance in the group. I. H. remarked that she was pleasantly surprised at how after some initial anxiety, he was able to participate actively and contribute to the group's discussion in a substantial manner.

Toward the end of the session, S. H. suggested that since the patient would be attending the group every week, the weekly individual sessions be decreased to twice a month. I. H. again protested that it was premature as Dan needed a great deal of support and direction at this time. S. H. again chided his colleague that she was underestimating the patient's strength, and in the end his decision prevailed.

In the next session, Dan reported that he had succeeded in renting an apartment with a partner and was in the process of looking for work as a security guard. S. H. expressed gratification that his faith in the patient was being rewarded. I. H. expressed surprise and admiration at the patient's achievements. However, she expressed concern that he was progressing at a very fast pace and was fearful that he would stumble and fall. She therefore suggested that he advance at a much slower pace (restraining) (Weeks and L'Abate 1982). This point of view was vociferously challenged by her colleague.

During the session, Dan raised the sensitive and painful issue of boy–girl relationships, explaining that on the one hand he felt lonely and wished to have a relationship, but on the other, was frightened and inexperienced in dealing with girls.

After focusing on the patient's feelings, fears, and expectations, S. H. suggested that Dan take upon himself the task of calling three girls for a date by the next meeting. It was explained to him that he needed to gain experience in arranging dates, and it was of secondary importance at this stage if he went out or not. Again, characteristically, I. H. protested that Dan was not yet ready for heterosexual relationships and expressed doubt about his ability to take on this assignment at this stage (defiance) (Weeks and L'Abate 1982).

In the following session, Dan appeared depressed and explained that none of the girls responded positively to his invitations. Both the therapists pointed out that he had accomplished the assigned tasks and that he was expecting too much of himself in such a short period of time.

During this session and many other sessions, Dan tended to return to his original and familiar refrain of being lonely, depressed, and messed up and began talking about his unfortunate past, failures, and injustices that he had experienced, something that he characteristically did when confronted with frustration, anxiety, and failure. The therapists interceded and interpreted his behavior as a wish to give up the struggle, regress, and return to the "air-raid shelter" below ground and they quickly directed his attention to the "ground floor."

Dan was again instructed to call up three girls for a date by the next session in order to gain further experience in speaking and arranging dates with girls.

At the following meeting, Dan with a big smile on his face, reported that he went out with two girls and had started to work as a security guard.

The seventh meeting took place after an absence of six weeks due to Dan's army reserve duty. He related that he had gone out with several girls in the interim, but was anxious and in conflict about the process of establishing a close heterosexual relationship, fearful of rejection and failure in any sexual contacts.

Both therapists at this juncture "normalized" Dan's anxieties and feelings and pointed out that he was going through a difficult process experienced by the majority of young adults at this stage of their development.

At the end of the session, S. H. suggested that in view of the patient's significant progress, evinced both by his functioning in the group and the outside world, the individual sessions be reduced to one a month. He explained to Dan graphically that in the last few months the "child" part of him had decreased while the "adult" part increased significantly. I. H. pointed out also that the patient's dependent pattern had decreased considerably, as demonstrated by the fact that he was able to think and act more independently (Berne 1964).

In the next session, the therapists were confronted with a dramatic and surprising reaction when it was suggested that the individual sessions be discontinued and that Dan continue only in group therapy. In a matter-of-fact manner, he volunteered that he was concerned that when under stress he was capable of committing suicide with the gun given to him in his security guard position.

I. H. interjected that it seemed that Dan was frightened about the possibility of terminating treatment and wanted to communicate to the therapists that he still felt in need of support and help. S. H. accepted his colleague's interpretation and suggestion that monthly individual sessions be continued until termination of therapy in three months.

The topic of termination was referred to occasionally by the therapists in a matter-of-fact manner as they conveyed to the patient their expectations that he would handle it without undue difficulty. In the last session the therapists shared with the patient their satisfaction with his significant progress in such a short period of time and their confidence that he would be able to continue to cope effectively without treatment.

In parting, the therapists invited Dan to contact them by telephone after the three-month summer recess, and bring them up-to-date regarding his final academic plans and social life.

Conclusion

This patient exemplifies a group of psychiatric patients who have a history of extensive treatments without any sustained improvement. These patients attach themselves tenaciously to mental health professionals, and treatment for them is an end in itself rather than a means to an end. Frequently they use treatment as a holding pattern and thus avoid any commitments or taking concrete action in their lives until they have "worked through" their problem.

With this group of patients, the therapeutic process can be more detrimental than beneficial, as it prevents them from developing autonomy, competence, and mastery over their lives (Frances et al. 1984).

The wisest recommendation with this type of patient may be no therapy at all or a brief intervention with the goal of weaning the patients from treatment and thereby avoiding turning them into iatrogenically infantilized patients.

References

Berne, E. (1964). *Games People Play*. New York: Grove.

Frances, A., Clarkin, J., and Perry, S. (1984). *Differential Therapeutics in Psychiatry: The Art of Treatment Selection*. New York: Brunner/Mazel.

Hoffman, S., Kohener, R. and Shapira, M. (1987). Two on one: dialectical psychotherapy. *Psychotherapy*, 24:212–216.

O'Connell, D. S. (1984). Promise of treatment as an opening strategy for psychotherapy. *Psychotherapy*. 21:473–478.

Travers, J. A. (1986). The interminable patient. *The Psychotherapy Patient 3(1)*:1–2.

Weeks, G. R., and L'Abate, L. A. (1982). *Paradoxical Psychotherapy: Theory and Practice with Individual Couples and Families*. New York: Brunner/Mazel.

8

Cotherapy with a Phobic Patient

SEYMOUR HOFFMAN AND RONIT HERZOG-BRONSKY

A phobia is a persistent and irrational fear of a particular object, activity, or situation. The phobic patient uses avoidance mechanisms, which are self-reinforcing as anxiety is relieved, in coping with feared stimuli.

Exposure is the most common and effective way of treating those phobias that are learned or conditioned fears, and this is usually accomplished by systematic desensitization, flooding, or paradoxical intervention (Reid 1989).

Phobias that have meaning beyond the anxiety they cause, that is, those that serve defensive purposes (defense against feared drives—aggressive or sexual impulses) are better dealt with by a traditional dynamic approach, at times in conjunction with behavioral and/or family interventions.

This chapter describes the treatment of a woman with claustrophobia by cotherapists who used desensitization and flooding techniques concomitantly.

Case Study

> Rachel, a 24-year-old married woman, applied to the counseling service because of intense fears of being in closed (and especially locked) places. Because of these fears, she avoided elevators (walked up four flights to her apartment), public lavatories, and outings that involved entering caves.

Rachel had a younger sister aged 15 who was also fearful of being alone in an elevator ("caught the disease from me"). Her relationship with her family (parents, sister, and husband of one year) is very good as "they are warm and supportive." Rachel's father was crippled in a traffic accident fourteen years ago and today functions minimally. Mother is described as a giving, fearful, anxious, and overly protective person with whom Rachel has a very close and dependent relationship.

Rachel views herself as a fearful person from birth. She decided only recently to seek help because she wanted to be free from fears before starting a family.

In the initial meeting, Rachel stated that she was not interested in long-term therapy but only in brief therapy that would focus on and help her overcome her fears. When asked how many sessions she had in mind, she stated "around ten."

In view of the client's strong motivation, ego strengths, and good functioning, the interviewer acceded to her request. However, he informed her that because he planned to work with a cotherapist, treatment would be restricted to five sessions. The interviewer went on to explain that in his experience with these problems, treatment is expedited when two therapists are involved, and that positive results could be achieved with her in a brief period of time if she was willing to work hard during and between sessions. The client nodded in agreement and a meeting was scheduled for the following week.

Treatment

In the initial therapy session, Rachel, at the request of the therapists, described and graded her fears on a scale of one to ten. The female therapist (R. B.) pointed out to the client that some of her fears were normal and universal and mentioned that she also feared entering caves and flimsy elevators. The male therapist (S. H.) suggested that the treatment efforts be directed to help Rachel overcome her fear of being in closed and locked places and explained that as she successfully accomplished these goals, she would notice positive changes in other areas of her daily functioning ("ripple effect"). The therapists emphasized that in view of her past and present accomplishments and behavior, they on the one hand did not agree with her proclaimed self-image of being a "rabbit," and on the other hand had no intention of attempting to fulfill her request to be a "lion" like her husband, but something in between.

S. H. at this point informed Rachel that in order for her to be able to overcome her fears, she had to know her enemy well. Instead of running away and avoiding her enemy, she had to meet and experience it up close. To accomplish this the therapist suggested that Rachel enter the clinic's small air-raid shelter and remain there for a period of time. Rachel turned pale and adamantly refused to heed the therapist's request. R. B. at this point intervened and suggested that she enter the room with the client to "check it out," while he closed the door from the outside. After they exited, Rachel related that this experience caused her anxiety level to go up to 7. S. H. insisted that this was not high enough for the client to know her adversary well and suggested that she remain in the shelter alone while they locked the door from the outside.

Noticing the client's increased anxiety, R. B. protested that her colleague's pace was too quick and instead suggested that first Rachel remain alone in the shelter with the door closed and she remain outside the door in constant communication with her. S. H. protested that his colleague was coddling the client but reluctantly relented at the end. After a short period of time the client exited and reported that her anxiety level shot up to 9. The therapists congratulated her on her achievements—raising her anxiety level and not running away. In this manner, the client was prodded and encouraged to take on more difficult, anxiety-provoking, and demanding tasks. At the end of the session, Rachel received compliments on her accomplishments and was encouraged to continue these exercises until the next meeting, in a week's time.

In the next session, Rachel appeared with a broad smile on her face and reported on significant gains in overcoming her fear of being in locked rooms. "I no longer feel like a 'rabbit' and as a result of my successes I feel stronger and more confident."

After being persuaded that Rachel was ready and motivated to work on her elevator phobia, the therapists accompanied the client to a nearby tall building with several elevators and proceeded to work in the same dialectical fashion described above. In the process of advancement floor by floor, one therapist remained on the entrance floor near the elevator, while the other therapist stationed himself on the target floor in order to receive the patient. When Rachel chose to close her eyes as a means of containing her anxiety, the therapists pointed out to her that this was an example of avoidance behavior. She was instructed to keep her eyes open during the elevator ride and in this way get a better view of her adversary, to which she agreed.

In the two sessions devoted to the elevator phobia, Rachel progressed quickly and received positive feedback from the therapists and family members.

In the fourth meeting, Rachel reported with great pride and satisfaction that during the past two weeks she had experimented with the help of her husband and succeeded several times in riding alone in elevators to the ninth floor. "I'm still anxious but I am able to overcome my fears." After receiving the congratulations of the therapists, Rachel stated that she felt she could continue on her own and was of the opinion that there was no need for further sessions. In response to the therapists' inquiry, the client said that treatment enabled her to discover herself and her latent strengths. "Today I know that I'm not a 'rabbit' and I don't have to be a 'lion.' In the past I ran away from things. Today I believe in myself."

When asked to comment on the treatment format, Rachel responded, "It was very effective. Treatment would have taken much longer if I had been alone with Ronit. Being alone with Seymour would have been unbearable. Ronit encouraged me while Seymour pushed me. I trusted Ronit almost from the beginning and Seymour only toward the end."

Rachel related that in the beginning it bothered and confused her that there were disputes between the therapists and that there wasn't one opinion, viewpoint, and approach. Afterward, she got used to it and took what seemed appropriate for her from both therapists. Toward the end of the session, Rachel commented, "When Seymour told me that treatment would involve five sessions I thought he was joking. Now I know he was right."

In spite of the fact that Rachel was entitled to one more session, the therapists accepted the client's decision to terminate therapy and informed her they were available in the future if she wished to consult with them.

In a follow-up phone interview two months later, Rachel informed the therapists that she was doing fine and was thinking of starting a family.

Discussion

The interviewer, by assuring the patient in the first meeting that her problems were not very serious and solvable in less time than she had expected (on condition that she worked hard during and between sessions), began the "seeding" process. As Lick and Bootzin (1975) concluded in their review of the literature, expectancy of improvement significantly contributes to treatment success. "Expectancy influences the change process by increasing treatment compliance and the tendency to test reality and gives self-reinforcement for improvement and modifying self-thoughts."

Throughout the therapy sessions, each therapist assumed a specific role agreed upon beforehand. The male therapist's role was that of the "flooder" and instrumentalist who directed the pace and goals of treatment while his colleague was the "desensitizer" and nurturer who accompanied and protected the patient through her "perilous" journey and looked after her emotional state and needs.

The former addressed the adult part of the patient and attempted to frustrate all attempts at regression, while the latter supported the patient's need at times to regress for brief periods of time.

The interactions also facilitated the externalization of the patient's internal conflicts and ambivalent feelings and enabled her to become more aware of her inner self. The female therapist by her continued reinforcement, support, and encouragement also prevented premature termination and strengthened the patient's sense of control and autonomy in the therapeutic process. Rachel had a choice to proceed at the pace of the "flooder" or "desensitizer."

As a result of the interplay between the cotherapists, the relationship, trust, and bond between the supportive therapist and patient were strengthened, as they both had a common adversary. This caused the patient to be more cooperative and amenable to the latter's suggestions and instructions.

Though treatment of phobias is generally carried out by one therapist, it was the authors' impression that the therapeutic change was expedited as a result of the simultaneous use of desensitization and flooding techniques by the cotherapists. Further experimentation using the above approach is suggested.

References

Lick, J., and Bootzin, R. (1975). Expectancy factors in the treatment of fear. *Psychological Bulletin* 82:917–931.

Reid, W. H. (1989). *The Treatment of Psychiatric Disorders*. New York: Brunner/Mazel.

9

Intervention by a Consultant to Overcome Therapeutic Impasse

SEYMOUR HOFFMAN, SHULAMIT GEDANKEN, AND EILEEN LAHAT

The use of consultants in medicine is a highly recommended and accepted practice. The consultant is usually brought in (1) for his specialized knowledge and what it adds to the management of a given patient, (2) to provide a second look at a primary physician's diagnosis, and (3) when the physician has lost his objectivity about a patient (Keith and Whitaker 1983).

In the psychotherapeutic profession, the use of a consultant is a less acceptable and common practice. Possible explanations for this situation are the issues of transference and confidentiality and the concern of the therapist that this may negatively affect the patient's trust and confidence in him.

It has been our experience that the appropriate use of a consultant, even on a one-time basis, in situations where the therapist is in doubt, frightened, in a one-down position in therapy, or confronted with a therapeutic impasse can significantly contribute to more effective and quicker therapeutic results.

Since the consultant functions with a unique capacity and freedom, as his involvement with the patient is brief and passing, he can be more objective, insightful, and free to act and say things that the primary therapist would hesitate or fear to do. The consultant can make outrageous interventions or suggestions, raise highly sensitive and painful issues, and be provocative in questioning the patient's motivation and capacity to benefit from therapy and change, without being concerned about future repercussions or the effect on their relationship (Papp 1983).

The consultant, after interviewing the patient, can reinforce and support, in an authoritative manner, the primary therapist's diagnostic impression, management, and treatment of the case, and thus strengthen the patient's confidence in his therapist. The consultant can express diametrically opposite views from that of the therapist in order to more effectively reflect the patient's ambivalent feelings and expand his perceptions of himself and of his surroundings (Hoffman et al. 1987, Chapter 1, this volume). The consultant, by taking a provocative stance, can also cause the resistant and hostile patient to redirect his antagonism and anger from the primary therapist toward the consultant and thus facilitate the strengthening of the patient–therapist relationship (Hoffman and Segal 1990).

Following are two examples of one-time interventions by a consultant in situations of therapeutic impasses, which enabled the therapists to continue their treatment of their individual patients in a more effective manner.

Case 1

> Mrs. A., a 38-year-old mother of three, applied to the clinic for help because of severe depression, socialization problems, lack of self confidence, and constant family conflicts. Her family conflicts primarily centered around her eldest son, who frequently accused her of keeping secrets and lying to him. During the course of therapy, Mrs. A. revealed to her therapist her "dark secret," that though on her I.D. card she was registered as Jewish, she was actually a Christian.
>
> After immigrating from Russia to Israel with her Jewish husband 15 years ago, Mrs. A. did not convert but conducted herself outwardly as a Jewish woman. Throughout the years, the patient felt that she was living a lie, was deceiving her children and friends, and feared that her secret would be revealed. As her eldest son approached the age of bar mitzvah, Mrs. A's anxiety, fears, and guilt feelings increased as did the tension between her and her children.

The therapist attempted in a supportive and sensitive manner to persuade the patient to reveal her secret to her children and thus remove the barrier of suspicion and distrust between them, but with little success. After several months of futile efforts, the therapist felt frustrated and despondent about the lack of progress and sought her supervisor's support to terminate therapy. The supervisor suggested that he be brought in on a one-time basis to evaluate the situation and after the therapist received the patient's permission, a joint meeting was scheduled for the following week.

In the meeting, the consultant-supervisor, an observant Jew who wore a skullcap and was knowledgeable in Jewish law and traditions, empathized with the patient on her difficulty and reluctance to reveal her true identity to her children. He pointed out to the primary therapist that according to Jewish law, the patient's children are not Jewish in spite of the fact that they have conducted themselves according to Jewish tradition all these years. He agreed with the therapist that the patient's "dark secret" created distance, distrust, and tension between mother and children. However, he was worried about the negative impact and effect the revelation of the secret would have on the emotional well-being of the children and on their relationship with their mother.

After deliberation between them, the therapist asked the consultant for his recommendations. After some pause, the consultant suggested that one way of softening the blow and rectifying the damage done would be to consider the option of conversion for the mother and children. To the surprise of the therapist, the mother responded positively to the suggestion. The therapist suggested that the patient discuss this issue with her husband and report back to her next week.

In the following meeting, the patient appeared more confident, alert, and relaxed and for the first time in half a year, she initiated the conversation. Mrs. A. reported that her husband supported the idea of conversion and that she planned to raise the issue with her children in the coming week. The therapist supported Mrs. A's decision and provided her with the name of a rabbi who was willing to explain to her the ramifications and process of conversion.

In the following session, the patient expressed the feeling that a great weight had been lifted from her shoulders, that she felt more confident and freer in her social contacts and her family relationships were warmer and more gratifying.

Therapy was terminated by mutual consent several weeks later.

Case 2

Mrs. B., a 25-year-old married college student, sought help at the clinic because of obsessional thinking, difficulty in making decisions, forgetfulness, poor concentration, intense feelings of jealousy and suspicion, and an overriding feeling of not living up to her potential.

In the first therapy session, the patient, a psychology major, insisted on "cognitive therapy," a diagnosis that could help her better understand herself, and an outline of the therapist's treatment program and approach. In the sessions, the patient spoke in generalities, frequently queried the therapist regarding the therapeutic model she was applying and generally avoided speaking about her personal problems, feelings, and conflicts.

On two occasions Mrs. B. spoke briefly about her family and her sense of loneliness as a teenager, but immediately redirected the conversation to the technical aspects of the therapy and expressed criticism and disappointment regarding its effectiveness and appropriateness to her situation. Attempts by the therapist to support, empathize, and reflect the patient's feelings evoked reactions such as "these things I could do myself." When confronted with her negativistic behavior and frequent absences, Mrs. B. insisted that the sessions were important and of value to her. At times when she was given interpretations, feedback, and direct messages from the therapist, the patient accepted them only to reject them in the following meeting.

In essence, the approach–avoidance behavior in regard to the therapist and treatment reflected the patient's lifestyle of obsessional doubting and ambivalence in her daily functioning.

The therapist considered making stronger and more direct confrontations, but because of the fragile and tenuous relationship decided against it. She also was aware of feelings of frustration, impotence, and anger regarding the patient and the need for an objective view and opinion regarding the therapy situation. Therefore, it was decided, in consultation with a senior colleague, to invite the latter, with the patient's agreement, to the following therapy session. The suggestion was enthusiastically accepted by Mrs. B. as she expected the meeting to be interesting and productive and that "finally she would be understood."

After listening intently to the patient's presentation of her problems and complaints, views, and expectations of treatment as well as the views of the therapist concerning the latter, the consultant opined that Mrs. B. was attempting to dominate and defeat the therapist. He also pointed out the similarity between this behavior and her relationships with her husband and close friends. In the end he concluded that the client was a "hard nut to crack" and expressed doubts regarding her motivation and ability to benefit from therapy at this time. He personally would have given up some time ago if he were her therapist, as she hadn't benefited at all from treatment.

The patient protested the consultant's remarks and insisted that she did benefit from the sessions as she had better understanding of herself.

The therapist admitted to the consultant that Mrs. B. was not an easy patient, but informed him that she was not yet ready to give up.

At the end of the session the consultant supported the therapist's views that the patients wish for "cognitive therapy" was the latter's attempt to avoid dealing with her emotional problems and to control therapy and encouraged his colleague to continue focusing on affective material in therapy.

In the following meeting, a dramatic change was noticed in the patient's appearance and demeanor. She arrived on time for the first time and displayed more softness and openness toward the therapist.

Mrs. B. expressed intense anger toward the consultant, as she expected to meet someone who would be on her side, who would understand, accept, and support her and not the therapist. She vociferously denied wanting to destroy her therapist or her husband and was insulted and hurt at being viewed by him as a "hard nut to crack." However, she was very much gratified by her therapist's declaration that she hadn't given up on her yet. Mrs. B. also related that, to her surprise, she became closer to her husband following the "difficult" session.

Toward the latter part of the sessions, the patient for the first time shared, in an emotional manner, intimate information regarding herself, her fears, failures, and a recent crisis that she underwent.

Discussion

In Mrs. A's case, because of the consultant's "specialized" knowledge and background, he was able to gain the patient's confidence and trust almost immediately. As Keith and Whitaker (1983) point out, "when a Catholic family is seen, we try to get a priest as a consultant" (See also Hoffman et al. 1990).

By joining and empathizing with the patient's fears, concerns and stance and supporting them in an authoritative manner, the consultant was in a favorable position to influence and suggest alternate ways to the patient to resolve her dilemma. The primary therapist's concurrence with her colleague's suggestion and supportive efforts helped the patient get out of her unfortunate position in a relatively brief period of time.

In Mrs. B's case, it appears that the consultant's intervention accomplished several goals: (1) temporary destabilization of the patient's rigid defensive system (denial, intellectualization, isolation, etc.); (2) support of the primary therapist's feelings that her patient was indeed very difficult ("therapist killer") and of her views and approach in treating the patient; and (3) strengthening the therapist–patient relationship and facilitating the development of a therapeutic alliance.

Also, the therapist was able, when confronted with the patient's rigid and highly defensive behavior, to "bring in" the consultant ("the consultant would view this behavior, interpret this remark," etc.) and make confrontations while, at the same time, not take direct responsibility for them. This fact enabled the therapist to feel less frustrated and impotent and more free and confident in her therapeutic work (Hoffman and Segal 1990, Chapter 6, this volume).

In the above examples, the one-time intervention by the consultant effected a turning-point in the therapy and enabled the continuation of treatment in a more productive fashion. The use of consultants on a one-time basis in specific situations is normative in our therapeutic work with individuals, couples, and families, and we have had positive experiences in working with therapists with various years of experience, disciplines, and orientations. The main factors in determining successful outcomes seem to be the appropriateness of the case, the timing, and the presence of mutual trust, respect, and cooperation between the primary therapist and the consultant.

We highly recommend its greater utilization in specific therapeutic situations.

References

Hoffman, S., Kohener, R., and Shapira, M. (1987). Two on one: dialectical psychotherapy. *Psychotherapy* 24(2):212–216.

Hoffman, S., Laub, B., and Zim, S. (1990). Collaboration of clergy and psychotherapists in treating psychiatric patients. *Israel Journal of Psychiatry and Related Sciences* 27(3): 180–185.

Hoffman, S., and Segal, H. (1990). Phantom cotherapist: treatment of a suicidal Arab by a Jewish therapist. *Journal of Contemporary Psychotherapy* 20(2):123–130.

Keith, D. V., and Whitaker, C. A. (1983). Cotherapy with families. In *Handbook of Family and Marital Therapy*, ed. B. B. Wolman and G. Stricker. New York: Plenum.

Papp, P. (1983). *The Process of Change*. New York: Guilford.

PART II
Families

10

Cotherapy with an Electively Mute Child

SEYMOUR HOFFMAN AND BRURIT LAUB

Elective mutism is defined as a selective refusal to speak, independent of intellectual endowment or neurological status (Hinsie and Campbell 1970). Children with this disorder generally have normal language skills and elect to restrict their verbal communications to immediate family members.

These children are generally excessively shy, socially isolated and withdrawn, clinging, negativistic, and use temper tantrums and other controlling or oppositional behavior in the home (*DSM-III*).

Electively mute children can be divided into two groups: (1) those who use refusal to speak in a coercive fashion to manipulate people and the immediate environment, and (2) those for whom speaking is sufficiently anxiety producing so the child chooses to remain mute (Friedman and Karagan 1973).

Rosenberg and Lindblad (1978) list the following observations regarding choice of symptom and underlying dynamics of electively mute children: (1) the child is extremely determined to hold onto his symptom and has an overwhelming need to control; (2) the symptom becomes an extremely effective passive-aggressive maneuver by the child and arouses extreme feelings of anger, frustration, and disappointment in the parents; (3) the home atmosphere is not conducive to expression of feelings.

Although the age of onset is usually before five, the disturbance may come to clinical attention only with entry to school. Therefore, the symptom may already be a routine of the child and more or less accepted by his surroundings. Even worse, it may have become integrated in the child's self-image and consequently become highly resistant to psychotherapy (Elson, et al. 1965, Mora et al. 1962, Wright 1968).

Treating elective mutistic children can be very demanding and discouraging and cause feelings of helplessness, frustration, and anger in the therapists (Ruzicka and Sackin 1974).

Reports of varying degrees of success and failure with different therapeutic approaches, including psychotherapy, psychoanalysis, hypnosis, behavior modification, family therapy, and combinations of the above, are reported in the literature (Browne et al. 1963, Meijer 1979, Sluckin and Jehu 1969).

Elson and his co-workers (1965) concluded that superficial counseling, suggestion, and exhortation were quite ineffective as were insight or uncovering psychotherapy. Nolan and Pence (1970) have reported success with behavior modification techniques, while Rosenberg and Lindblad (1978) concluded that family therapy is always indicated in cases of elective mutism. In their view, the combination of a family and behavioral approach is essential in helping to remove the symptom of elective mutism in children and that either approach alone produces limited success. This combination, they feel, seems to ameliorate the symptom and change the dynamics that allowed for the development of the symptom. Continuing work with the family, according to them, also seems to serve to solidify the changes that have occurred in the child.

The literature on the treatment of elective mutism tends to focus on the anxiety or family dynamic component of the symptom and little attention is directed to the controlling, manipulating, negativistic, passive-aggressive component. As a result, the utilization of paradoxical interventions in the treatment of this symptom has received little attention.

The following case history describes a case of elective mutism treated successfully by the authors using paradoxical interventions in the context of a polarization model of cotherapy, in combination with behavioral techniques in a family therapy framework.

Case Study

Lily, a 4½-year-old kindergarten girl, was referred to the clinic because of her refusal to speak to adults, with the exception of her parents and four grandparents. In school she spoke only with the children and used her closest friend as an intermediary when communicating with the teacher.

Lily's family consists of parents, age 30, and a 7-year-old brother named Eli. At approximately age 2, Lily was hospitalized for two weeks because of a serious case of ataxia. The parents described the hospitalization as traumatic both for them and for the child, even though the child recovered quickly. The parents reported that from that time on, Lily refused to talk and avoided contact with adults, although even before that time she had tended to cry when grownups outside the immediate family approached her. The referring psychologist, who had treated the family for a year using a "structural family therapy approach and educational guidance," described the child as possessing at least average intelligence.

Before the initial meeting with the family, the authors decided to avoid getting into a power struggle with the child (and continue to do "more of the same") and to relate to her in a totally different manner than, we presumed, she anticipated. In the first session, after the formal introductions, the therapists informed the parents that they do not speak to young children and that if they wished to tell Lily something (or she them), the therapists would use the parents as intermediaries. Throughout the first and subsequent meetings, Lily attached herself to her mother and avoided contact with the therapists.

In the third session, the therapists expressed their belief to the family and to the two sets of grandparents, who had been invited to that meeting, that Lily had a good reason for refusing to speak to adults although they themselves were not certain of the reason. Several hypotheses were offered: her speech was infantile and, therefore, she was afraid that adults outside the immediate family constellation would laugh at her; or that she felt that the family wanted an infant in the house; or that it could be her way of uniting the entire family by having them preoccupied with her "disability"; or it could be her way of notifying the family that she did not wish to grow up and leave the warmth and security of the home. In this meeting the therapists also emphasized the importance of ceasing to pressure her to speak to adults (the grandfather, for example, had promised her an expensive talking doll if she spoke to adults). Following this meeting, the therapists met with the kindergarten teacher and received her promise to cooperate in not pressuring the child to speak to her.

In subsequent sessions with the nuclear family, there developed a contrived split between the two therapists. The "bad" male therapist took the stance that Lily was an infant and, therefore, was not able to speak to adults, and that it was important to the family that she remain this way since the parents did not plan to have any more children. The "good" female therapist, in contrast, expressed the belief that Lily was capable of mature behavior and encouraged the family to start relating to her in accordance with her age. The "good" therapist lavishly praised the child and parents when they reported that their daughter began eating by herself, helped with the dishes, and so on. The male therapist continued to express doubt about the child's achievements and pointed to her clinging and childlike behavior in the room as proof that she was an infant.

In the following session Lily refused to enter the office, and in contrast with previous times, the therapists permitted the behavior. During the middle of the session the female therapist left the room to answer the telephone and exploited the situation to whisper several words to the child and to give her a hug. When the female therapist returned, the male therapist sent Eli out with a message to his sister that he did not believe the parents' report that she put together a fifty-piece puzzle by herself, because little children are not able to do such a difficult task. The brother returned with his sister's response, "The psychologist is an idiot." This was the first obvious breach in the child's detachment facade and armor.

At the next meeting, Lily presented to the therapists via the parents a picture of a fruit tree that she had drawn. Though the therapists both admired the drawing, the male therapist expressed doubt that she had drawn it since she was so immature, while the female therapist and family members insisted that she did draw it and that she was capable of mature and age-appropriate behavior. The parents also pointed out that the kindergarten teacher was also impressed by the child's artistic ability.

An argument ensued between the therapists regarding the child's ability to speak maturely. The male therapist insisted that she was only able to babble and make sounds like aah, baa, vaa, daa, and so on, while the female therapist insisted that she was capable of mature speech. They decided to bet 100 shekels on who was right, and told the family that they would return in a few minutes and listen to the tape that they had inserted in the tape recorder to determine who won the bet. After hearing the child's voice on the tape, the male therapist grudgingly gave a 100 shekel bill to his cotherapist, even though he protested that Lily's speech was not very loud or clear and did not give evidence that she was able to speak in full sentences. At this point, the female therapist asked the father to bring to the next session a tape recording of Lily speaking, to which he acceded.

After hearing the child's voice on the tape at the following session, the male therapist admitted that he had erred, but still insisted that she was immature in that she was not able to speak in the presence of adults not of the immediate family. He then challenged Eli to bet him candies on whether Lily would be able to speak in the presence of the female therapist after he absented himself from the room. The female therapist expressed confidence that Lily would be able to accomplish the task and Eli agreed to the bet. Upon hearing Lily's voice on the tape recorder after returning to the office, the male therapist reluctantly placed candy in the hands of the smiling children. The defeated therapist, however, persisted and challenged Eli again to bet him on whether his sister would be able to speak directly even one word to the female therapist in his absence. He again accepted the challenge, but this time lost the bet as Lily was only able to open her mouth, but could not emit any words. The male therapist gloated over his victory and collected his prize from the dejected children.

At the end of the session, the male therapist proclaimed that his primary interest was to acquire as much candy as possible and was unconcerned whether the girl spoke or not, and in a provocative manner challenged Eli to a further bet. The therapist took out a bag of candy and said that if Lily would speak one word to the kindergarten teacher by the time they returned to the next meeting the candy would be theirs. A letter from the teacher attesting to this was required. If not, they would have to give him a bag of candy. Again the female therapist expressed confidence in the child's ability to succeed in this assigned task and after agreeing to the bet, Eli was given the bag of candy for safekeeping.

Several days later, the father appeared unexpectedly with a large grin on his face, shook the male therapist's hand, kissed the female therapist, and with great emotion revealed that Lily not only spoke to the kindergarten teacher but also to other adults. We smiled approvingly and told him the children could eat the candy to celebrate their victory. We cautioned him however, to relate to this new phenomenon in a natural manner.

In the final session, the eighteenth, the parents presented the therapists with chocolate and a small celebration was held, which was the culmination of a long chain of festivities sponsored by the kindergarten teacher and various family members. The celebrations reminded us of a bat mitzvah ceremony (when a Jewish girl reaches the age of adulthood and responsibility), as if Lily had received the family's permission and blessing to grow and mature. The grandmother of the child exclaimed to the female therapist whom she met several days later, "It's coming to me a *mazal tov*" (congratulations).

In response to the female therapist's question, the child explained that the reason she did not speak to adults in the past was that she had a sore throat and last week it stopped hurting. The therapists noted that the bag of candy that she won was still unopened as if the child was going to hold on to her "trophy."

At the end of the session, the male therapist apologized profusely to the child for thinking that she was an infant and asked for her forgiveness. Lily timidly shook the therapist's extended hand, and thus accepted him to the list of adults with whom she conversed.

In a follow-up meeting two months later, the parents reported that Lily had stopped using a pacifier, extended the list of adults with whom she speaks, expanded her circle of friends in kindergarten, and was displaying more independent and age-appropriate behavior.

Discussion

In the case of Lily, two components of the elective mutism symptom were present—anxiety and control. While the former may have been central at the beginning, it appears that the latter component became more prominent after a while as a result of secondary gains obtained from the environment.

In view of the aforementioned, we elected at the beginning of the treatment process to use a paradoxical approach that included redefining the symptom and refraining from attempting to remove it.

As a result of these interventions, the decreased attention given to the symptom and increased provocations on the part of the male therapist, Lily was "unbalanced" and the effect and strength of her symptom was diminished significantly. To reestablish and regain power and control, the child had to prove to the male therapist that he erred. Had she refused to take part in the "gambling game," it would have been an admission that he was right and that she was truly a helpless infant who was incapable of speaking to adults. The "triumph" over the male therapist regained for her the control and power but in a more constructive and appropriate way.

The stance taken by the "good" therapist was directed primarily at decreasing the anxiety component of the symptom through actions aimed at strengthening self-confidence and self-esteem, while the position of the "bad" therapist was primarily directed toward the control/defiance component of the symptom through the use of defiance-based paradoxical interventions. The male therapist's provocative behavior also angered the child and thereby forced her to become involved in the therapy sessions.

The positive attitude of the female therapist enabled Lily to continue attending the sessions and to begin experimenting with age-appropriate behavior. The provocations of the male therapist indirectly encouraged the child to "join" the "good" therapist in order to defeat the "bad" therapist. At this point, behavioral techniques such as reinforcement, counterconditioning, and successive approximations were effective in decreasing the child's anxiety in regard to speaking to adults.

The father, who was an electrician by trade, explained the therapeutic process in professional terminology. While there was a positive connection between Lily and the female therapist, there was a short circuit between her and the male therapist. In reference to this, the father related that Lily was extremely upset and furious at the male therapist's remark that he was only interested in acquiring candy and not in whether she spoke or not. This provocation caused her to speak to the kindergarten teacher and to other adults to prevent him from winning more candy and to prove him wrong.

The father concluded that there was a need for a plus and minus in the therapeutic situation to induce an electrical current (change of a static situation). Two pluses ("good" therapists) or two minuses ("bad" therapists) would not have produced, in his view, the same results.

It should be noted that the above case report focused only on the treatment of the elective mutism symptom and did not include the process of family therapy that also dealt with other problems presented by various family members.

References

American Psychiatric Association. (1980). *Diagnostic and Statistical Manual of Mental Disorders, 3rd ed.* Washington, DC: American Psychiatric Association.

Browne, E., Wilson, V., and Laybourne, P. C. (1963). Diagnosis and treatment of elective mutism in children. *Journal of the American Academy of Child Psychiatry* 2:605–617.

Elson, A., Pearson, C., Jones, C., and Schumacher, E. (1965). Followup study of childhood elective mutism. *Archives of General Psychiatry* 13:182–187.

Friedman, R., and Karagan, N. (1973). Characteristics and management of elective

mutism in children. *Psychology in the Schools* 10:249–252.
Hinsie, L. E., and Campbell, R. J. (1970). *Psychiatric Dictionary, 4th ed.* London: Oxford University Press.
Meijer, A. (1979). Elective mutism in children. *Israel Annals of Psychiatry and Related Disciplines* 17(2):93–100.
Mora, C., Devault, S., and Schopler, E. (1962). Dynamics and psychotherapy of identical twins with elective mutism. *Journal of Child Psychology and Psychiatry* 3:41–52.
Nolan, J., and Pence, C. (1970). Operant conditioning principles in the treatment of a selectively mute child. *Journal of Consulting and Clinical Psychology* 35:265–268.
Rosenberg, B. J., and Lindblad, M. B. (1978). Behavior therapy in a family context: treating elective mutism. *Family Process* 17:77–82.
Ruzicka, B., and Sackin, H. (1974). Elective mutism: the impact of the patients' silent detachment upon the therapist. *Journal of the American Academy of Child Psychiatry* 13:551–561.
Sluckin, A., and Jehu, D. (1969). A behavioral approach to the treatment of elective mutism. *British Journal of Psychiatric Social Work* 10:70–73.
Wright, H. L. (1968). A clinical study of children who refuse to talk. *Journal of the American Academy of Child Psychiatry* 7:603–607.

11

Cotherapy with a Case of "Matricide"

BRURIT LAUB AND SEYMOUR HOFFMAN

Two of the basic tenets of the practice of prescriptive eclecticism in psychotherapy are (1) the psychotherapist must be able to draw upon a vast array of theory and techniques and not be bound by a single approach to therapy, and (2) the therapist's task is to construct an individualized psychotherapeutic program that will match the client's needs and situation (Dimond et al. 1978). The following is a case study that reflects these points.

Case Report

Presenting Problems

The patient, a 27-year-old bachelor, accompanied by his father, appeared at the clinic with the following complaints: shortness of breath, pains in his chest and legs, decreased functioning at work, poor concentration, an overpowering feeling that he is "going crazy" from his constant thoughts regarding the death of his mother, and suicidal thoughts.

Though he had been suffering from these complaints for the past five years, the patient acceded to his father's pleas to seek help only because of his deteriorating condition.

The patient attempted to hold back tears as he related the incident that took place ten years ago that dramatically altered his life.

His mother, who suffered from several serious illnesses and whose mental condition was far from stable, expressed a desire to end her life. One day the patient found her attempting to hang herself in the washroom and severely chastised her. Later that day she poured gasoline over herself and repeatedly asked her son to light a match in order to help her die. After failing to persuade her to remove her gasoline-soaked clothing, the patient, in an effort to appease her, lit a match and immediately smothered the fire. When his mother continued to nag and taunt him to light another match, the patient repeated the act, but this time was unsuccessful in putting out the fire immediately. As a result, despite his family's efforts, the mother received serious burns on most of her body. In the hospital, the mother took responsibility for the act and stated that she wanted to live, but because of her generally poor physical health, she died the following day.

Patient's History and Family Background

The patient is the younger of identical twins. His brother is married and the father of a girl, while his sister, who is ten years his senior, has three children. His father, a former concentration camp inmate, had a stormy strife-ridden marriage and frequently sought succor in extramarital affairs. The late mother was described as a warm, overprotective, and strong woman who was expert at hurting people in their vulnerable areas.

The patient was viewed as a sensitive, weak, and fearful child who was very attached to and dependent on his brother and mother. The parents encouraged the strong bond between the brothers, and the twins were always together, from kindergarten until they went into the army. Today they work for the same company and see each other daily at work and several times during the week in the evening. The older brother took care of the younger sibling throughout the years, even to the extent of going out with a girl and presenting himself as his brother in order to "break the ice" for him. All the family members live near each other and are very much involved in each other's lives.

When the older brother married, the patient reacted with anger and hostility toward his wife. Both brothers viewed the marriage as a "betrayal," and as if to reassure him that things had not changed, the older brother invited his twin to accompany them on their honeymoon, which he declined. In a short time, the patient accepted his sister-in-law and thereafter found a significant place for himself in their lives. As his brother stated in one of the sessions, "My brother takes first place in my life, even before my wife and child. We are one body."

Six months ago the patient established a relationship with a woman, with whom he shares his apartment, but not his "awful secret." The patient feels that he cannot marry and bring children into the world because, as he said, "I will make my family miserable."

It is important to note that around the time of the brother's marriage, five years ago, a co-worker of the patient hanged himself after a disappointing flirtation with a married woman. This incident seems to have triggered the patient's symptomatic behavior.

Treatment

At the therapist's request, the patient came alone to the second meeting. In that session he spoke freely about his ambivalent feelings toward his mother: on the one hand he felt very close to and dependent on her, while on the other he resented and hated her for her provocative and unpredictable behavior. He felt he could not live a normal life because of his overwhelming guilt feelings over the "act," which occupied him day and night. An attempt to relate his guilt feelings to his suffering and symptoms (self-punishment) produced little reaction from the patient.

In the next session the patient appeared with his twin brother, whom he had invited without prior consultation with the therapist. The patient's brother spoke of the close ties among family members and especially between himself and his brother, and how they all had attempted to free the patient of his sense of guilt and responsibility for the tragic incident, but with little success.

The therapist was impressed by the strong symbiotic ties among the family members and speculated that the patient's symptoms and suffering might be serving the goal of maintaining the family closeness and unity (in light of the threat of dissolution as a result of the marriages of the father and brother). In view of this, the patient was asked to return the following week with his nuclear family and was informed that a female cotherapist would also participate in the session (Hoffman and Gafni 1984, chapter 2, this volume).

Family Sessions

Ten family meetings were held, two of which included the spouses of the family members. The patient was asked to bring his girlfriend, but he refused. In the first meeting, the patient's sister declared that his symptoms were unrelated to the tragedy. She saw the patient as egoistic, unable to make decisions by himself, and full of complaints, just as the deceased mother had been. In her view, the patient was using the symptoms as an excuse for his inability to be independent and get married.

Recall of the tragedy revived much anguish and anger in the family. At one point, the father said that after they had put out the fire, he had yelled at his wife, "What did you do to your son? You destroyed his life. This will be on your conscience. You killed yourself and him!"

In following family sessions, various structured interventions were used to destabilize and undermine the enmeshed structure of the family (e.g., raising conflicts, requesting less family involvement in each other's affairs, viewing the patient as strong and self-sacrificing rather than weak and dependent) in order to foster greater differentiation and more autonomous behavior (Minuchin 1974). An attempt also was made to restructure the family boundaries and hierarchies—to change the daughter's status from "mother surrogate" to that of daughter and sister, and strengthen the subsystems of the father and his wife, the sister and her family, the brother and his family, and the patient and his girlfriend.

A noticeable change occurred in intrafamily relationships as a result of these interventions. The relationship between the daughter and father improved and there was a decrease in the overinvolvement with and overprotective behavior toward the patient and his symptoms on the part of the family members. However, little change was effected in the symbiotic ties between the twins (Adelman and Mari 1986).

In the tenth session, the family members united against the therapists, insisting that the treatment was superficial and irrelevant and that the patient's presenting problems were being ignored. After consulting briefly with each other, the therapists decided to ask the patient to come to the next session by himself.

Individual Sessions

In the following session the therapists raised the issue of the severity of the matricidal act and the accompanying guilt feelings. In contrast with the family members' reactions, the therapists insisted that this was a very serious offense. However, they took a polarized position as to the significance of the offense (Hoffman and Laub 1986, chapter 10, this volume). This was done to promote externalization of internal dilemmas and ambivalencies of the patient and thus make them more available for therapeutic work and resolution (Hoffman et al. 1987, chapter 1, this volume).

The male therapist (who wore a skullcap) attempted to represent the stern, rigid, and uncompromising superego of the patient by emphasizing that the patient's symptoms and suffering were legitimate expressions of his guilt feelings and self-punishment for the anger and death wishes harbored toward his mother and for the horrible deed he had committed. The female therapist, on the other hand, agreed that the offense was serious but had been unintentional, and that, even more, according to the family's story, the mother had exploited the patient in getting him to help her end her suffering. He had been angry with her, but he also had loved and pitied her. At the end of the session, the patient exclaimed, "Finally you're on the right track. You understand me."

The two therapists deliberated between themselves regarding the possibility of atonement for the patient. The male therapist suggested consulting a religious authority, and the patient, though not religious himself but of a traditional background, agreed. However, he requested that the therapists speak to the rabbi first to prepare him for the "shocking" story.

In the initial meeting with the rabbi, the psychologists presented the patient's history and the purpose of the upcoming meeting. The rabbi, a respected and recognized Torah scholar, was chosen because of his psychological sophistication and experience in counseling students and members of his community.

At the patient's request the meeting was held in a synagogue in the presence of the two psychologists (Seltzer and Seltzer 1983). After hearing the patient's story, the rabbi stated that the offense committed was indeed very serious. He proceeded to explicate on Judaism's view of the sanctity of life and then read several select portions from Maimonides on repentance. The rabbi then concluded: "According to the Torah, you are obliged to believe that nothing stands in the way of repentance and this includes even the serious offense that you have committed. I am also not convinced that all the responsibility for the offense falls upon you, in view of your mother's erratic and disturbed behavior. The Torah requires that the penitent go through a process of experiencing and suffering guilt feelings and regret for the offense committed, a process that you have undergone more than required, and it is a pity that it has continued for so long. By your preoccupation with the offense, you are perpetuating it. You are now required to pass on to the second stage of identity change, doing good and charitable deeds. It seems to me that you can realize identity change by getting married and having children. By naming your child after your deceased mother you will be perpetuating her memory for generations."

At the conclusion of the session, the rabbi instructed the patient to donate money to a worthwhile charity in his mother's name, to visit her grave, and in the presence of family members pronounce the new path that he was taking.

In the following session, the patient mentioned that the meeting with the rabbi had had a strong impact upon him. However, in his view "nothing had changed."

It was the therapists' impression, however, in spite of the patient's disclaimer, that positive changes had taken place. The patient appeared less despondent and distressed, had ceased referring to his somatic disorders, and in the last session, spoke of future vocational plans. However, he was not confronted with these observations.

The patient was given the written opinion of the rabbi as he had requested and was instructed to take it home to study. He was told that it might take him a while to digest the significance of the meeting and the contents of the letter, and that he should contact the therapists when he felt ready for the next meeting.

Three months later, the therapists called the patient for a follow-up meeting at which he related that two weeks after the meeting with the rabbi, he saw a "rosy path," but afterward returned to his regular style of life and did not act upon any of the rabbi's recommendations. He again expressed the feeling that he was carrying the "mark of Cain," and was pessimistic about the effectiveness of treatment. At this point, feeling stuck and frustrated at the lack of further progress and change in the patient, the therapists left the room to discuss the matter. They concluded that in order for change to occur, the static relationship between the patient and his girlfriend had to be jarred. This, it seemed, could be most effectively accomplished if the patient's girlfriend was told his secret.

Upon resumption of the session, the patient was asked, "Suppose you revealed your secret to your girlfriend; what do you think would happen?" (Penn 1982). He responded that if their relationship deteriorated in the future, she might use it against him. "If this incident had happened to my father, my mother would definitely have exploited it."

The therapists redefined the patient's problem as "marriage phobia," which was a result of the influence of his parents' terrible marriage. They emphasized the importance of his working on this problem with his girlfriend.

To help the patient overcome his ambivalent feelings and resistance to sharing his secret with his girlfriend, the therapists again took opposing positions. The male therapist argued that the patient feared his girlfriend would leave him if she knew the circumstances of his mother's death and therefore he dared not reveal it to her. The female therapist argued that this was an important test for both of them. If his girlfriend was not able to accept him with all that had happened, it was best that he know about it. She pointed out that although there was risk involved, it was also an opportunity, and since it was a difficult and important decision, he would need several weeks to consider it. At this point, the male therapist confronted his colleague: "You relate to him as if he is a child, a cripple, just as his family relates to him." At this, the patient attempted to appease the therapists: "It will be all right. I'll tell my girlfriend and I don't need several weeks to decide." He then gratuitously offered an explanation for the opposing views of the therapists: "Since you're a woman, you can be soft, and since you're a man, you have to be hard."

In the next session, the patient informed the therapists that at his request, his sister had revealed the secret to his girlfriend. The therapists expressed satisfaction at the turn of events and asked the patient to invite the girlfriend to the next meeting, to which he agreed.

At the next and final session, the patient's girlfriend substantiated the therapists' impression that the "secret" had caused a stalemate in their relationship. Once it was revealed, the couple became closer and the patient, for the first time, said that he loved her.

The girlfriend mentioned that she saw the patient as a strong, responsible, independent, and sensitive person, who was capable of making decisions. There was only one area in which he could not decide—marriage—because he was "stuck." She also mentioned that throughout their relationship, she had been working on lessening his strong ties to his family, with some slight success. Marriage and the rearing of children, in her view, would gradually free the patient from his preoccupation with his mother's death.

At the end of the session, the therapists expressed their opinion that the patient was in good hands and that there was no need for further sessions. They asked to be sent a wedding announcement and wished the couple well.

Follow-up Information

A follow-up telephone interview was conducted with the couple several months later. Though the patient stated that he was "feeling 100%" and "nothing had changed," his girlfriend reported that in the past few months their relationship had deepened, that the patient was more open and relaxed, his mood more positive, and that she was more optimistic about future marital plans. A half year later the therapists attended the couple's wedding, officiated by the aforementioned rabbi.

References

Adelman, M. B., and Mari, S. (1986). Communicating the relational shift: separation among adult twins. *American Journal of Psychotherapy* 40(1):96–109.

Dimond, R. E., Havens, R. A., and Jones, A. C. (1978). A conceptual framework for the practice of prescriptive eclecticism in psychotherapy. *American Psychologist*, 33(3):239–248.

Hoffman, S., and Gafni, S. (1984). Active interactional cotherapy. *International Journal of Family Psychotherapy* 6:53–58.

Hoffman, S., Kohener, R., and Shapira, M. (1987). Two on one: dialectical psychotherapy. *Psychotherapy* 24:212–216.

Hoffman, S., and Laub, B. (1986). Paradoxical intervention using a polarization model of cotherapy in the treatment of elective mutism: a case study. *Contemporary Family Therapy* 8(2):136–143.

Minuchin, S. (1974). *Families and Family Therapy*. London: Tavistock.

Penn, P. (1982). Circular questioning. *Family Process* 21(33):267–280.

Seltzer, W. J., and Seltzer, M. R. (1983). Magic, material and myth. *Family Process* 22(1):3–14.

12

Cotherapy with Anorexic Families

SARA GAFNI, BRURIT LAUB, AND YAEL LAVIE

The professional literature describes various therapeutic approaches to anorexia—psychodynamic (Bruch 1978, 1985), behavioral (Halmi 1985), cognitive behavioral (Garfinkel and Garner 1982, Garner and Bemis 1985), family systemic (Caille et al. 1977, Minuchin et al. 1978, Palazzoli et al. 1987, White 1983), and pharmacological (Garfinkel and Garner 1982)—in different settings: individual, family, or group, and in- and outpatient arrangements (Garfinkel and Garner 1982, Garner and Bemis 1985). Today there is a move toward eclecticism (Dym 1985, Garfinkel and Garner 1982, Goldfried 1980, Kalucy et al. 1985). Individual-oriented psychodynamic therapists admit the need to include the family in the treatment (Bruch 1985); family therapists resort to behavioral techniques, especially during the initial stage of weight gain (Minuchin et al. 1978, Sargent et al. 1985); while behavioral therapists concede the need for combining their techniques with individual counseling and family therapy (Halmi 1985). Other therapists have pointed out the limitations of family therapy in those cases where individual psychotherapy is indicated in order to change intrapsychic attitudes (Kalucy et al. 1985).

The mode of intervention described here relates to the central problems of the anorexic disturbance: the need for control (Bruch 1978, Minuchin et al. 1978), fear of the consequences of physical growth and mature development (Garfinkel and Garner 1982), and conflict-avoidance patterns (Minuchin et al. 1978). Our model is based on work using the active-interactional cotherapy approach (Hoffman and Gafni 1984, Chapter 2, this volume), in which two therapists, in overt interaction with each other, concentrate on the "here and now"—expressing, in the presence of the patient, their thoughts, emotions, and attitudes. The therapists utilize modeling, role play, paradoxical interventions, polarization (taking opposing attitudes on significant issues), and sometimes alternate between consent and disagreement (Hoffman and Laub 1986, Chapter 10, this volume, Laub and Hoffman 1987, Chapter 11, this volume, Solomon and Morrison 1972). Somewhat similar approaches have been described in the family therapy literature (de Shazer 1977, Papp 1980, Sheinberg 1985).

Attention is paid to personal and interpersonal conflicts, in the process of externalization, emotional processing, and reinternalization, in order to achieve integration at a higher functional level for both the individual and the family. Typically, conflicts concern issues of control, dependence, autonomy, individuation, and femininity.

The redefinition of the anorexic symptom by the two therapists facilitates expression of the problems on two different levels. The "supportive" therapist places greater emphasis on the interpersonal, family aspect and regards the symptom as a voluntary act of control—similar to Minuchin's approach. The "challenging" therapist, however, relates more to the intrapersonal aspect, emphasizing the sense of lack of control and helplessness of the anorexic—similarly to the approach of Bruch.

The Therapeutic Process

The model proposed here was successfully applied in the therapy of several families of anorexic girls. The girls, ages 12 to 17, were in an acute ano'rexic state, less than two years after commencement of symptoms. Therapy took place in an outpatient clinic, in collaboration with a physician when necessary.

Stage 1: Redefinition of the Symptoms by Cotherapeutic Dialectic Interaction

At the beginning of therapy, the problem is redefined as one of control, the therapists taking opposing attitudes. The challenging therapist relates to lack of control by the anorexic girl, while the supportive therapist relates to her ability to control the situation.

The challenging therapist claims that, in the girl's present state, even if she wanted to, she would be unable to eat. This therapist points out that the side effects, such as lack of concentration, weakness, fatigue, chills, and headaches, are well-known symptoms of people suffering from starvation, and emphasizes the irreversible physiological damage. Thus, the therapist proposes that, due to her present physical condition, it is impossible to rely on her understanding, judgment, or assurances, as was the case in the past. In this therapist's opinion, there would be no chance for her to get out of her current condition by herself.

The supportive therapist takes a completely different position. In the supportive therapist's opinion, the girl is in control of her situation, and is able to terminate the self-starvation at any time she chooses. Her behavior actually demonstrates impressive self-control, since it is so difficult for anyone to stop eating so effectively.

The therapists discuss termination of the fasting, both agreeing that it is *imperative* for the girl to commence eating and gain weight immediately. While the supportive therapist thinks that she could succeed by herself, the challenging therapist disagrees openly, rejecting this premise.

Later in the session, the therapists invite all members of the family to join the debate and express their opinions. It should be noted that the therapists do not comply with the family's demand to investigate the reasons behind their daughter's anorexia.

Stage 2: The Parents as a Therapeutic Team

The challenging therapist places sole responsibility on the parents for their daughter's health, and demands that they ensure her weight gain by whatever means. This pressure forces the parents to bring into the open their disagreement on the way to deal with the problem. Typically, their relationship reveals a mutual disqualification, with one of the parents taking an assertive stance, while the other negates this stance (Boscolo et al. 1987, Selvini-Palazzoli 1974).

The challenging therapist joins forces with the more assertive parent, often entering into open confrontation with the "protective" one. The therapist emphasizes the common responsibility of both parents for their daughter's condition—that only their mutual cooperation will ensure success of the treatment. The supportive therapist, who until this point encouraged expression of the girl's independence and competence, gradually starts to support the position of the challenging therapist, and to agree with the necessity for a cooperative effort from both parents.

Stage 3: Finding Alternative Modes of Coping with the Problem

At this stage, the focus of treatment shifts from the anorexic condition to the uncovering of conflicts related to control, autonomy, dependence, individuation, and femininity—utilizing common methods of family therapy (Minuchin et al. 1978, Sargent et al. 1985).

Case Illustrations

Case 1

> Ronit, aged 12, was referred by a physician in the children's ward of a hospital after a weight loss of ten kilograms (twenty-two pounds) over the previous six months. The self-starvation process began, according to her parents, after Ronit's girlfriend told her that she was getting fat. Ronit began to examine herself in front of the mirror after each meal, became introverted and despondent, and suffered from insomnia. Ronit's condition caused her mother to become very worried, whereas her father became angry.
>
> At the first meeting, Ronit appeared thin, hunched up, and underdeveloped. She gazed into space, was introverted, and did not reply when questioned. She was described as being a perfectionist, a good student, and exhibiting devotion and responsibility toward her four younger sisters—yet there was competition between her and her brother, who was one year older.
>
> It was possible to discern from the mother's report that there were latent disagreements between the parents. The mother claimed that her indulgent approach encouraged Ronit

to eat, whereas the father's approach only caused tension. The therapists made it clear that the therapy should include the whole family.

Ronit refused to talk during the second meeting as well. The therapists told her that it would be acceptable if she did not speak, but that when questioned, she should simply nod or shake her head if her answer was "yes" or "no."

The father dominated the conversation; the mother was quiet and passive. He was angry with Ronit, who had caused him to neglect his parents and become more involved with problems at home.

After each of the family members described how he or she saw the problem, the two therapists agreed and emphasized that Ronit's condition was grave and should be considered an emergency—it was absolutely imperative that she gain weight.

The supportive therapist said that it was Ronit's decision to eat or not, and if she should decide to eat, she would be able to do so. The supportive therapist added that this was her way of showing her dissatisfaction with the fact that her brother "deserves everything." Ronit feels that she cannot talk to her family about her difficulties, so she remains silent.

The challenging therapist disagreed with the supportive therapist: Ronit was in such poor condition—psychologically and physically—as a result of her fasting that she was simply incapable of thinking and knowing what was happening to her. She had lost the ability to decide whether or not to eat; even if she should decide to eat, she would be unable. At the moment she was like a baby, incapable of looking after herself, and she should not be considered as a mature person. If she wanted to draw attention to the situation at home, there were other, more productive ways of doing so.

The supportive therapist expressed astonishment at the views of the challenging therapist—Ronit could, of course, stop fasting whenever she wanted. After all, she had decided to lose weight, and succeeded. If she decides to gain weight, she will definitely do so. Further evidence of her willpower and control is the fact that she had been able to bring all of her family to therapy.

The challenging therapist replied that although Ronit might have a great deal of power, in her present condition she is unable to use it because she has totally lost control of herself. The parents are the ones who should help her and are capable of doing so, because they are the adults and responsible for their children. The challenging therapist turned directly to Ronit, asking, "Who is right? It's me, yes?" Ronit answered by shaking her head "no."

The same question was addressed to the other members of the family. Her sisters did not give a clear answer. Her brother said that Ronit was acting spoiled. Her mother said that Ronit could gain weight—that she is responsible and can be trusted. Her father said, "Perhaps Ronit can eat, but at the moment she is incapable of being responsible for herself."

At the next meeting, Ronit's mother reported that she had been eating more. Indeed, she looked better; she also participated in the session. The supporting therapist responded with enthusiasm and inquired about her weight gain. It turned out that she had, in fact, lost an additional half kilo (one pound).

The challenging therapist turned to Ronit's mother and to the supportive therapist in amazement: "One thing I fail to understand—how can it be that Ronit ate, yet continued to lose weight?" The question caused some embarrassment. The father came to his wife's defense, saying that he too had seen Ronit eating, but he thinks that she had not eaten enough because her mother is too compliant and indulgent. In his opinion, the solution to the problem was to put pressure on Ronit—not to give in to her.

The challenging therapist turned to Ronit's mother and said, "It does not matter how and what Ronit eats. What is important is that she gains weight. Today Ronit needs help; she is not capable of looking after herself. You are her mother and you must help her before it is too late." The therapist added, "If her condition does not improve, we will have no choice but to have her hospitalized."

Two weeks later, Ronit's parents reported that she had gained one kilogram (over two pounds). Ronit was open and cheerful and spoke freely. The conversation shifted to her social and family difficulties, her desire for leadership, to be an example to her younger sisters, and her fighting with her brother who tries to dominate her. At the same time, Ronit's mother described her disappointment with her husband's role at home, asking him directly to give a helping hand. Other subjects that arose during therapy were the father's anger and criticism leveled at his son, competition between Ronit and her brother, competition between the parents for greater esteem in the eyes of the children, and links with the parents' families of origin.

On completion of therapy, which lasted three months (seven sessions), Ronit gained weight and recovered from her anorexic condition, improved socially, and related better with her brother and sisters. Her parents were able to discuss conflicts and problems between themselves in a relatively open, direct fashion, and father and son became closer. Follow-up two years later indicated that Ronit had maintained the improvements gained through therapy.

Case 2

Orit was 14 years old when she was referred to therapy. She had lost eleven kilograms (over twenty-four pounds) in one year of dieting and had developed amenorrhea.

Orit's maternal grandmother, who had been widowed during the Second World War and had raised her three children by herself, also took part in some of the sessions. There were obvious disagreements between Orit's parents, the father taking a rigid, pedantic attitude that caused the rest of the family to fear him, while the mother was indulgent and soft. In spite of this, the household seemed to be run in accordance with the mother's wishes. At the beginning of therapy, they presented their daughter's eating problem as the only family problem, and they returned to this position repeatedly afterward. Both parents agreed that Orit had to eat, the father demanding that a firm position be taken. However, the mother, who pitied Orit, established an indulgent approach. The grandmother, while agreeing with the father's approach, actually supported the mother by her actions.

During therapy, the coalition between Orit and her 15-year-old brother—who gave her a great deal of support—became obvious. Together they pointed out what their mother had not mentioned—their difficulty in dealing with the overriding domination of their father. After intervention, as per the model described earlier, a change in the patterns of interaction within the family was noted. Orit gained weight only after her mother was able to change her approach, taking responsibility and being more assertive. The changes in the attitude of the mother brought her closer to her husband's position, allowing him to soften his approach, and permitting both of them to find a way of cooperating. Orit began taking an interest in her feminine appearance in spite of her father's opposition, and later her relationship with her peers also improved.

Attempts were made to bring up additional problems for consideration, such as the father's feelings of loneliness and difficulty in dealing with three women in the household (even his own son did not support him), as well as behavior problems of the son at home. These attempts, however, were curtailed at the outset.

At the last meeting (eighth session), the father reported that Orit had gained weight, and since that was the sole reason they had come, the family had decided to terminate therapy. Orit showed continued development at the two-year follow-up.

Discussion

In this chapter, a model of cotherapy suited for intervention in anorexic families was presented. It was used because, in our estimation, it matches the structure of the anorexic family problem.

This therapeutic model emphasizes the direct responsibility of the parents in terminating the anorexic symptoms of their daughter. Restoring the capacity of the parents to assume responsibility allowed for a clear distinction between parent and child subsystems:

1. The parents learned how to cope as a team with problems arising among their children, as opposed to the previous condition, which was characterized by overinvolvement of

one parent with the identified patient and by latent conflicts between the parents.

2. The parents, who had lost their confidence when faced with their daughter's deteriorating condition, learned anew to trust their own powers and competence (Haley 1980). This contrasts with approaches that remove responsibility from the parents, which is the case when the patient is hospitalized (Kaufman and Sadeh 1989), or when emphasizing individual therapy (Bruch 1978, 1985).

In the initial stage, the anorexic condition is redefined as a problem of control (Minuchin et al. 1978). But in this model, it is raised through dialectic interaction, which has the following advantages:

1. Polarization of the therapists' positions traps the patient in a position where she is forced to question her self-image. Previously, she tried to prove her self-control by starving herself. Now, to prove that she is indeed in control of the situation and that the supportive therapist's assumptions are correct, she must start eating. If she continues to starve herself, she proves that the challenging therapist is right in claiming that she is weak and helpless.
2. The polarization and open argument between the therapists allows for expression of the patient's internal conflicts relating to control and lack of control, strength and weakness, dependence and independence.
3. The polarization between the therapists also serves to uncover the opposing attitudes of the parents, particularly with regard to their daughter's ability to begin eating. The example of therapists openly expressing opposing views legitimizes the parents' own disputes, and can be used as a model for their ability to cooperate.
4. The anorexic family views matters in a one-dimensional manner. The patient can either be looked upon as being very successful (premorbid condition), or as weak and in need of protection (the morbid condition). The polarization of the therapists imposes upon the family a multidimensional view of the situation. It demonstrates the possibility that both weakness and strength can coexist. The opposing positions

of the two therapists, expressing strength and weakness, enable the family to renounce their denials and change their one-dimensional perception to one that is relatively more integrated.

5. For the anorexic family, characterized by conflict avoidance (Minuchin et al. 1978), this model offers a framework for meeting and dealing with conflicts in an open, direct manner. In the course of the argument between the therapists, the individual family members are forced to take a clear stand.

In the second stage of the therapeutic intervention, a parallel process takes place. The therapists' authority vis-à-vis the parents is paralleled by the ensuing parental authority over their daughter. Development of the parents' autonomy through recognition of their role as parents, and through their ability to act on that role, discontinue overinvolvement with their daughter, and reduce the competition between themselves, as well as set aside their fears of being "bad," also allows their daughter to achieve autonomy and assume responsibility.

These stages include elements of surprise, exaggeration, dramatization, and directness, which are utilized to create a therapeutic impact (Minuchin and Fishman 1981, Omer 1987).

During the third stage, after emerging from the acute crisis, intervention is aimed at the realization of the possibilities of individuation and growth in each of the family members by finding alternative modes of coping. Immediate and direct intervention, along with an emphasis on the urgency of the situation, keeps it from becoming chronic (with intermittent hospitalizations) by exerting pressure on the family to change their rigid patterns of interaction.

Intervention is carried out at the level of the family and its environment. Instead of enlisting outside help, family members, preferably the parents, are called on to help. The girl remains within her normal environment, thus preventing regression, psychic trauma, and the social stigma of hospitalization.

Significant points include the following:

1. It was necessary to take a clear and firm position in the face of the parents' repeated attempts to bring only part of the family to therapy.

2. Special awareness and sensitivity was needed in order to recognize subtle attempts at manipulation, which is characteristic of anorexic families. In these situations, it was most important to have two therapists present.
3. Family members who fear conflict, and who have difficulty expressing their feelings openly, generate an impression of emotional shallowness, similar to the effect of having taken tranquilizers. Such a response can either lull the therapists or make them angry.
4. In most cases, the families we treated discontinued therapy at their own initiative when the girl gained weight and her social condition and family functioning improved. The desire to discontinue therapy generally arose when the issue of interparental conflict came under investigation. Nevertheless, most families continued therapy as long as they were stuck in the developmental stage of granting autonomy to their adolescent children. When they overcame this barrier and progressed, therapy was no longer deemed necessary. The families taught us to accept and respect the limits of change that were suitable for them.

References

Boscolo, L., Cecchin, G., Hoffman, L., and Penn, P. (1987). *Milan Systemic Family Therapy.* New York: Basic Books.

Bruch, H. (1978). *The Golden Cage: The Enigma of Anorexia Nervosa.* London: Open Books.

——— (1985). Four decades of eating disorders. In *Handbook of Psychotherapy for Anorexia Nervosa and Bulimia*, ed. D. M. Garner, and P. E. Garfinkel. New York: Guilford.

Caille, P., Abrahamsen, P., Girolami, C., and Sorbye, B. (1977). A systems theory approach to a case of anorexia nervosa. *Family Process* 16(4):455–465.

de Shazer, S. (1977). The optimist–pessimist technique. *Family Therapy* 4(2):93–100.

Dym, B. (1985). Eating disorders and the family: A model for intervention. In *Theory and Treatment of Anorexia Nervosa and Bulimia*, ed. R. S. W. Emmett. New York: Brunner/Mazel.

Garfinkel, P. E., and Garner, D. M. (1982). *Anorexia Nervosa: A Multidimensional Perspective.* New York: Brunner/Mazel.

Garner, D. M., and Bemis, K. M. (1985). Cognitive therapy for anorexia nervosa. In *Handbook of Psychotherapy for Anorexia Nervosa and Bulimia*, D. M. Garner, and P. E. Garfinkel. New York: Guilford.

Goldfried, M. R. (1980). Toward the delineation of therapeutic change principles. *American Psychologist* 35:991–999.

Haley, J. (1980). *Leaving Home*. New York: McGraw-Hill.

Halmi, K. (1985). Behavioral management for anorexia nervosa. In *Handbook of Psychotherapy for Anorexia Nervosa and Bulimia*, ed. D. M. Garner, and P. E. Garfinkel. New York: Guilford.

Hoffman, S., and Gafni, S. (1984). Active interactional cotherapy. *International Journal of Family Therapy* 6(1):53–58.

Hoffman, S., and Laub, B. (1986). Paradoxical intervention using a polarization model of cotherapy in the treatment of elective mutism: A case study. *Contemporary Family Therapy* 8(2):136–143.

Kalucy, R. S., Gilchrist, P. N., McFarlane, C. M., and McFarlane, A. C. (1985). The evolution of a multitherapy orientation. In *Handbook of Psychotherapy for Anorexia and Bulimia*, ed. D. M. Garner, and P. E. Garfinkel. New York: Guilford.

Kaufman, M., and Sadeh, T. (1989). Anorexia in the kibbutz: Factors influencing the development of a monoideistic fixation. *International Journal of Eating Disorders* 8(1):33–53.

Laub, B., and Hoffman, S. (1987). A multimodal psychotherapeutic approach to a case of "matricide." *Family Therapy* 14(1):35–42.

Minuchin, S., and Fishman, H. C. (1981). *Family Therapy Techniques*. Cambridge, MA: Harvard University Press.

Minuchin, S., Rosman, B. L., and Baker, L. (1978). *Psychosomatic Families*. Cambridge, MA: Harvard University Press.

Omer, H. (1987). Therapeutic impact: A nonspecific major factor in directive psychotherapies. *Psychotherapy* 24:52–57.

Palazzoli, M. S., Boscolo, L., Cecchin, G., and Prata, G. (1987). Family rituals: A powerful tool in family therapy. *Family Process* 16:445–453.

Papp, P. (1980). The Greek chorus and other techniques of paradoxical therapy. *Family Process* 19:45–57.

Sargent, J., Liebman, R., and Silver, M. (1985). Family therapy for anorexia nervosa. In *Handbook of Psychotherapy for Anorexia Nervosa and Bulimia*, D. M. Garner, and P. E. Garfinkel. New York: Guilford.

Selvini-Palazzoli, M. (1974). *Self Starvation*. London: Chaucer.

Sheinberg, M. (1985). The debate: A strategic technique. *Family Process* 24(2):259–271.

Solomon, A. P., and Morrison, D. A. R. (1972). Anorexia nervosa: Dual transference therapy. *American Journal of Psychotherapy* 26(4):480–489.

White, M. (1983). Anorexia nervosa: A transgenerational system perspective. *Family Process* 22(3):255–273.

13

Cotherapy with "Marital Phobia"

SEYMOUR HOFFMAN AND LEAH ROSMAN

In strategic psychotherapy, the therapist formulates a plan in advance and acts on it to resolve the presenting problem(s) of the client as quickly and effectively as possible (Haley 1963). Strategic therapies do not assume that change depends on the achievement of insight or emotional release, nor are their goals to explicitly promote the growth and development of the client. The objective is to solve problems through minimal but sufficient interventions so that the clients can get on with life (Rohrbaugh and Eron 1982). The following is a case study of the treatment of "marital phobia" using a strategic therapeutic approach.

Case Study

Presenting Problem

Dona, a 37-year-old single woman, telephoned to request an urgent meeting, saying that her boyfriend of three years had decided to terminate their relationship just after she had raised the issue of marriage. She was very upset, as their relationship was very close and mutually satisfying. In her view, her boyfriend had a serious psychological problem, since he had reacted similarly four years ago when his previous girlfriend proposed marriage.

A meeting was scheduled for the couple the same week. Dona was informed that a female cotherapist would participate in order to increase the effectiveness of the meeting.

Background

Dona and her boyfriend Eli, who is four years her senior, are both observant Jews and school teachers. Dona lives alone while Eli lives with his widowed mother in his apartment.

Eli is the youngest of six children. From the age of seven, he lived in a dormitory and received a religious education. He recalled that there was much tension between his parents and that his father was a weak person while his mother suffered from bouts of depression, especially after his brother was killed in an automobile accident several years ago. She was also overly preoccupied with cleanliness and the state of her health. Eli's father died of a heart attack fifteen years ago.

Treatment

In the initial meeting, Dona spoke in a free, spontaneous, and at times emotional manner, while Eli was circumscribed, cautious, and stilted in his speech and behavior. The couple described their relationship as very good and mutually rewarding. They see each other several times a week, speak every day on the phone, have similar interests and values, and enjoy each other's company. Because of religious constraints, they have not indulged in sexual relations.

Eli revealed that he experienced chest pains, sweating, shortness of breath, and other physical symptoms after Dona spoke of marriage. Since he could not honor her request, he decided to terminate the relationship in spite of his feelings for her. He explained that he could not marry Dona because he was not sure that she was an appropriate mate for him due to her age and the fact that at times she did not appear attractive to him.

The cotherapists decided to use a prearranged active interactional approach to reflect, clarify, and externalize Eli's inner ambivalence and conflicts and thus make them more available for treatment. The male therapist took the position that Eli's physical symptoms might be a warning not to make a quick and dramatic change in his life. The female therapist, on the other hand, interpreted Eli's physical reactions as natural and normal responses to a highly significant and emotional situation. This approach was used throughout the session as the therapists raised and focused on important and sensitive issues. Toward the end of the session, Eli remarked, "You are excellent actors. You are also highly professional people." Dona nodded in agreement. Eli volunteered that the therapists' interventions helped him to better recognize and understand his anxieties and conflicts. This was in sharp contrast to his first therapeutic experience, which he had undergone after terminating the relationship with his former girlfriend.

The therapists decided to invite Eli for another meeting to further evaluate his situation (O'Connell 1984). Dona was instructed to refrain from raising the issue of marriage until the assessment procedure was completed.

In the next meeting, Eli reported that there was no change in his psychological and physical condition. The therapists were impressed by his passivity, evasiveness, and emotional detachment as they attempted to explore the underlying reasons for his anxieties and distress. They offered possible explanations for his high state of tension and somatic complaints, such as his concern about losing his independence, his fear of responsibility, of making a commitment, of failure, of fatherhood, of sterility, his sexual anxieties, difficulty in separating from his mother, and the fact that he had poor role models at home. Eli rejected all these possibilities but was not able to suggest alternatives.

In the following sessions, an attempt was made to help Eli cope with his anxieties regarding marriage through the use of guided imagery (Morrison 1981). This was unsuccessful, as Eli experienced difficulty imagining the situations suggested by the therapists. In view of the client's fear of self-exposure, limited insight, and passive-resistance to change, Madanes' (1981) strategic intervention, "pretending," was considered as a way to circumvent the client's rigid defensive structure.

In the next meeting, to which Dona was invited, the therapists acknowledged their disappointment and frustration in not being able to help Eli overcome his problems. In their view, two possibilities remained: (1) to help Dona gradually leave Eli or (2) to have the couple participate in a "pretending" exercise. This would require Eli to pretend that he was free from his anxieties and fears regarding marriage and thus enable him to marry Dona. It was explained to them that the purpose of this exercise was to help determine the dire consequences and changes that might occur as a result.

Before the therapists left the room, they asked the couple to discuss the two options and make a choice (Breit et al. 1983). After deciding on the second option, they were given a written homework assignment to be completed by the next visit. The assignment involved jointly discussing and deciding on a wedding date, gown, ring, hall, ceremony, officiating rabbi, guest list, apartment, honeymoon, and other matters related to getting married.

In the following meeting, the couple reported that they had carried out the assignment. After perusing their work, the therapists awarded them a high mark. Eli volunteered that the task had been very difficult and at one point he had been tempted to flee the situation. The therapists congratulated him on his perseverance and encouraged him to continue with the assignment until all the marriage details were worked out.

Toward the end of the session, the therapists explained to Eli that he was suffering from "marital phobia" and that his anxieties and somatic complaints were the by-products. They pointed out that they had successfully treated various kinds of phobias such as agoraphobia and school phobia and related problems such as test and crowd anxiety, and that they could help him reduce and control his distress through a relaxation procedure. To this end, he was invited to another meeting and asked to bring along a blank cassette.

As a result of a positive experience with the relaxation procedure, Eli requested another session for the same week. He explained that he was going abroad the following week and wanted to "better equip" himself with the relaxation exercise before he departed. The female therapist agreed, but the male therapist said that since Eli was being provided with tools to reduce and control his anxiety and tension, it was time that he "stepped into the water," that is, that he and Dona set a definite and realistic date to get married and stop the "pretending game" (the "pretend date" had been set for two weeks hence). Visibly pale and tense, Eli meekly agreed to consider the request.

In the next meeting, Eli reported that after a lengthy discussion with Dona, they had decided on a wedding date three months hence. He added that following the last session, he felt more anxious and got through the week only with difficulty.

Eli continued to respond positively to the relaxation exercise and was given a tape of the session so that he could practice during his trip. It was agreed that Eli would contact the therapists upon his return to arrange for future sessions.

Several weeks later, Eli called to inform the therapists that he was doing fine and did not feel the need for further sessions. He requested the addresses of the therapists so that he could mail them wedding invitations.

Two months later, the therapists attended the wedding. Six months after the wedding, in a chance meeting with one of the therapists, Eli reported that he and Dona were happy and doing fine.

Discussion

To help this anxiety-ridden, highly defensive, poorly motivated, and passively resistant client to overcome and cope with his fears and conflicts, several strategic techniques and interventions were employed in a brief but intensive therapy:

1. Before initiating therapy, the client was informed that he would have to undergo a process of evaluation to determine his problems, whether he could be helped, and if so, the best approach to take. This "promise of treatment" (O'Connell 1984) as an opening strategy permitted covertly therapeutic experimentation and possible problem resolution without potential for failure. It also intensified the client's response to any eventual treatment.

2. The active interactional approach facilitated the externalization of the client's internal conflicts and ambivalence, thus making them more accessible to treatment.
3. By diagnosing the client's complaints and giving them a name (Torrey 1972), he was provided with something that he could "hold onto" (especially important in view of his obsessive-compulsive and intellectual defenses and need to be in control). This, together with the therapists' assurance that they had successfully treated similar problems, increased the client's confidence in the therapists and in the treatment procedure, thus reducing his resistance.
4. Since people generally find choice more palatable than mandate, the "illusion of alternatives" strategy provided this choice to the client in a way that bypassed his resistance. By making a choice, the client assumed responsibility for his behavior, thus channeling his oppositional behavior into constructive directions.
5. The "pretending" exercise enabled the client to "expose" himself and experience the feared situation without the accompanying overwhelming anxieties and somatic reactions. In this way, he was able to increase his self-confidence, control his fears and the environment, and even develop an interest in experimenting further. Pretending also implicitly dissociates the client's ego and behavior, which reveals that one has a degree of control over that behavior.
6. Last, by providing the client with tools for reducing and controlling anxiety through relaxation exercises, a sense of self-respect, independence, competence, and mastery was restored.

References

Breit, M., Won-Gi, I., and Wilner, S. (1983). Strategic approaches with resistant families. *American Journal of Family Therapy* 11:51–58.

Haley, J. (1963). *Strategies of Psychotherapy*. New York: Grune and Stratton.

Hoffman, S., Kohener, R., and Shapira, M. (1987). Two on one: Dialectical psychotherapy. *Psychotherapy* 24(2):212–216.

Madanes, C. (1981). *Strategic Family Therapy*. San Francisco: Jossey-Bass.

Morrison, J. K. (1981). The use of imagery techniques in family therapy. *American Journal of Family Therapy* 9:52–56.

O'Connell, D. S. (1984). Promise of treatment as an opening strategy for psychotherapy. *Psychotherapy* 21(4):473–478.

Rohrbaugh, M., and Eron, J. B. (1982). The strategic systems therapies. In *The Newer Therapies: A Sourcebook*, ed. L. E. Abt, and R. I. Stuart. New York: Van Nostrand Reinhold.

Torrey, E. (1972). *The Mind Game: Witchdoctors and Psychiatrists.* New York: Bantam.

14

Marital Cotherapy

SEYMOUR HOFFMAN AND SMADAR BEN-DAVID

The active interactional cotherapy approach described here has been used in group (Hoffman and Segal 1989, chapter 15, this volume) and individual therapy (Hoffman and Merdler 1988, chapter 4, this volume). It involves two therapists who, from the beginning of treatment, take consistent opposing roles and views of the patients. By directly presenting to the patient his/her "divided self," the patient can be brought to grasp and deal with underlying conflicts, distorted perceptions, and ineffectual behavior (Hoffman et al. 1987, chapter 1, this volume).

Haber and Cooper-Haber (1987), in the treatment of a couple, adopted a position along a change/no change continuum of a systemic symptom in order to induce the couple to function in a less predictable way, thus increasing the chance of a more creative solution to the systemic impasse.

The therapeutic approach with couples presented here involves two therapists who attempt to provide to the discontented couple a clear picture of their "divided marital dyad" in a direct, forceful, and quick way. This is accomplished by each therapist assuming the role of "lawyer" or "mouthpiece" for his/her "client," thereby enabling both sides to better understand and appreciate his/her better half, fears, conflicts, wishes, ambivalencies, and aspirations. In this approach, highly emotionally laden, conflictual, and meaningful material can be introduced early in the sessions, and an assessment of the marital situation and therapeutic goals, whether in the direction of helping the couple to improve or to dissolve their marriage, can be more quickly and effectively realized.

Since the therapists are in an adversarial relationship, they are in a position to present a positive model for the battling couple—two adults who are not always in agreement, interacting with each other in an open, mature, and constructive way. They can also make use of their relationship to show the couple how to communicate clearly, and as a result, produce a more functional relationship (Dowling 1979).

Case Study

David and Ruth, a young couple in their mid-twenties, were referred for marital counseling by David's therapist. David recently terminated a year of individual therapy and in light of his progressively deteriorating marital situation, his therapist recommended marital counseling.

David and Ruth had been married for three years, after an off-and-on relationship for four years. They did not have any children and had been living apart when they appeared for the initial interview.

David's motivation for couple therapy was strong; he intensely missed his wife and wanted her back immediately. Ruth, on the other hand, was very hesitant about marital therapy; she was confused and uncommitted to her marriage and was working on these and other issues with her private therapist. She agreed to the meeting only after David threatened divorce proceedings if she refused.

Ruth had left David suddenly two months ago because she felt a need to be alone in order to assess her marital situation and to experience an independent life.

During the session, areas of conflict were raised, such as sexual dissatisfaction, poor communication, and conflicting values and personality makeups. At the end of the interview, the therapist suggested that another meeting be held that would include a female cotherapist to help assess and clarify the marital situation. The couple agreed and an appointment was scheduled for the following week.

In view of the highly unstable situation (David's and Ruth's goals were dissimilar—David was interested in working to improve the marriage, and Ruth was interested in exploring her feelings regarding her husband and the marital situation), a quick, direct, and intensive intervention seemed indicated in order to uncover the dynamics, hidden issues, and conflicts.

At the meeting, Ruth aired her complaints regarding David—he was too intellectual, he was not emotional, he was weak and gave in too readily, and did not satisfy her sexually. David's main complaint was that Ruth was highly critical and controlling at times.

The therapists raised questions regarding the present separation: How long was it to last? What were the rules? (e.g., Were extramarital relationships acceptable?). David insisted on a clearly defined time limit and was against extramarital relationships for either of them, while Ruth could not commit herself to a definite time limit and was against restrictions on extramarital relationships.

At one point, when David was adamantly insisting that Ruth return home immediately, the male therapist interjected that Ruth needed distance and privacy in order to straighten out her inner turmoil. The female therapist, on the other hand, shared David's pain and distress over being abandoned, and his feeling of frustration and anger because she was making all the decisions. It was as if she was keeping him on a "back burner." David nodded in agreement at these observations, as if finally finding that someone understood him.

The therapists returned to the issue of the rules of the separation, emphasizing the importance of an immediate resolution. Ruth responded by saying that she felt she had to be honest, revealing that she recently had had an intimate relationship with a man. She explained that she needed to find out whether her inability to reach orgasm was her own or her husband's fault, and was relieved to find out that it was David's.

David was stunned and hurt and unable to speak for a few minutes. Ruth stated that she did not want to hurt David, that her relationship with him was important to her, and that she wanted to work on improving their marital and sexual relationship. In response to the therapist's inquiry, she responded that she was not willing to give up her extramarital relationship at that time. The therapists were united in their view that it was not possible to help her improve her marital relationship as long as she was involved in another relationship. They suggested that she consider this point, and in spite of David's feelings that there was no reason for another meeting, an appointment was scheduled for the following week.

In the third session, David arrived late and was silent for the first few minutes. Ruth complained that there had been no contact between them even though she had attempted to indicate to David that she wanted to be with him. David expressed anger at Ruth for treating him like a doormat, noting that he had conceded his interests, hobbies, and independence out of fear of losing her—that he loved his wife while she did not love him. Ruth countered that she lacked self-confidence and needed him. David interpreted this as another example of exploitation and not love.

The therapists focused on the couple's different views of the word *need* as it was reflected in their personalities and styles. Ruth is the "poetess," with strong proclivities toward spiritual and emotional aspects of life, while David is the scientist, the organized intellectual with a need for an exact understanding of things. It seems that the qualities they lack, they seek and find in their spouse. The couple readily accepted these observations. As to whether they would make the same choice again, David said he would, while Ruth had doubts, which hurt David.

The female therapist volunteered that David is an emotional person, since he speaks of love and feelings for his wife. The male therapist stated that David's feelings are covered by intellectual wrappings and thus not readily visible. It seemed to him that Ruth was more vulnerable since she lacked these wrappings. Ruth concurred with this assessment, while David was surprised to see another aspect of his wife. Instead of the strong-willed, dominant, critical, and controlling woman, he was able to see, for the first time, the frightened, insecure, and needy woman behind the persona. The therapists pointed out that in view of their different personalities and styles, they had to become sensitive to each other's language.

In the fourth session, the therapists continued to confront their "client's" spouse, raising pertinent questions and issues while encouraging both parties to participate in the discussions. Toward the end of the meeting, David expressed the feeling that the female therapist understood him: "She is like a video of my feelings. She reflects exactly what I feel."

In the fifth meeting, David complained that one hour a week was insufficient to work on their problems, especially when they were living apart without contact between them. The therapists agreed, but had different solutions to the problem. The female therapist supported David's view and insisted the couple had to live together so they could work on their relationship. The male therapist countered that Ruth's need for her "private life space" had to be respected, and that they could work on their relationship by increasing their contact with each other between sessions.

The female therapist suggested that the reason Ruth left David was that she felt too dependent on him and wanted an opportunity to learn to become more self-sufficient. Besides her problems with David, she had problems of her own. David accepted this but insisted that he also had feelings and needs.

Toward the end of the session, David said he was frustrated and disappointed in the therapy sessions and wished to terminate the meetings and the marriage. Ruth expressed anger and impatience with David, and concurred that there was no reason for further meetings.

At this point, the male therapist requested that the couple participate in a brief "experiment" called the Hand Contact Test. He asked Ruth to place her hand on David's for two minutes, and then made the same request of David. They were to be quiet and keep their eyes closed. After the experiment, the couple was asked for their reactions. Ruth said that it had been a pleasant experience and that she had felt warm and safe. David said that he did not feel anything. The male therapist observed that when David's hand was on top, he made movements to envelop his wife's hand, while Ruth's hand was stationary in both positions. David acknowledged this and stated that he wanted the closeness, but was afraid to betray his feelings. The female therapist pointed out that though Ruth enjoyed the experience, she did not give any outward evidence of this.

A final meeting (summation) was scheduled for the following week in spite of the couple's pessimism regarding the continuation of their marital relationship. Several days later, Ruth called to cancel the appointment, explaining that she and David had had a long discussion and had decided to get a divorce. She thanked the therapists for their efforts and for their offer of future help if they should be in need of it.

Discussion

Based on the initial interview and clinical impression, the cotherapists decided that the female therapist would represent the husband, and the male therapist the wife, since in their judgment the former needed the respect and support of a sensitive woman, which he lacked, and the latter needed the alliance and understanding of a strong male figure, which she lacked.

Both therapists attempted to provide support and show the various aspects of the personality makeup and behavior of their respective "client." They also served as a "mouthpiece," raising sensitive issues and verbalizing feelings and thoughts that the spouses avoided expressing. Though the ending was not "and they lived happily ever after," it was felt that this therapeutic approach enabled each partner to become more aware of his or her own dynamics and conflicts, as well as those of the spouse and the marital dyad, and to respond more appropriately.

References

Dowling, E. (1979). Cotherapy: A clinical researcher's view. In *Family and Marital Psychotherapy*, ed. S. W. Skinner. London: Routledge and Kegan Paul.

Haber, R., and Cooper-Haber, K. (1987). Paradox and orthodox: A cotherapy approach. *Journal of Strategic and Systemic Therapies* 6(2):41–50.

Hoffman, S., Kohener, R., and Shapira, M. (1987). Two on one: Dialectical psychotherapy. *Psychotherapy* 24:212–216.

Hoffman, S., and Merdler, A. (1988). Use of dialectical psychotherapy in treating bulimarexic disorders: A case study. *Journal of Contemporary Psychotherapy* 18(3):93–102.

Hoffman, S., and Segal, S. (1989). Dialectical approach in group therapy. *International Journal of Group Psychotherapy* 39(3):413–418.

PART III
Groups

15

Group Cotherapy

SEYMOUR HOFFMAN AND SARIT SEGAL

In this chapter the application of the active interactional cotherapy approach with a group is described with examples of how several significant issues were handled by the cotherapists.

Case Study

The group consisted of nine college students who applied to the university's counseling service for help with various problems, which included social anxiety, lack of self-confidence, fear of establishing close relationships, difficulty in assertive behavior, family conflicts, and dependence–independence issues. Weekly sessions of seventy-five minutes were held throughout the academic year.

In the group sessions the issue of active member participation was raised. Several of the group members were actively involved in the group discussions, raised issues, problems, conflicts, gave feedback, and interacted with the other group members, while others sat passively and were minimally involved in the group, in spite of the efforts of the group leaders.

The male therapist raised this issue in a metaphoric way. He pointed out that everyone paid his entrance fee but only a few were making use of the pool. Several people entered the deep water, others the shallow water, while others were sitting on the side in their bathing suits and still others were wearing their street clothes. Everyone came here to learn to swim and to do that one had to enter the water.

The female therapist countered that everyone had to enter at her own pace. By paying the entrance fee and appearing at the pool they had indicated their interest in learning to swim. Some may be waiting because the water was too cold while others preferred observing the action in the pool in order to gain courage to join in.

The above dialogue prompted a heated discussion between the group members. Several members wanted to oust the ones who were still in "street clothes," insisting that they didn't fit in the group. The male therapist stated that he could understand their anger and resentment since they took the risk while others did not, while his cotherapist argued that one had to be patient and give support to the "nonbathers."

Issues regarding fear of exposure and rejection, peer judgment, poor self-image, lack of self-confidence, and difficulties in establishing interpersonal relationships came to the surface at this as well as at future meetings. The male therapist characteristically took a provocative and challenging role in these discussions, while his colleague took a supportive and encouraging one.

For example, the former insisted that the "nonbathers" should at least take a symbolic step to indicate their sincerity in joining the others by "removing some of their outer clothing." The female therapist at this point, encouraged the "nonbathers" to share some personal though not necessarily intimate information with the group and with some difficulty and hesitancy they acceded to her request. This intervention was used several times during the group sessions with considerable success.

Another topic that was raised on several occasions was the issue of assertiveness and the expression of anger. In one of the sessions, a rather diffident member mentioned that he was hurt and angry at another group member because of his (rather mild) critical remarks. The female therapist remarked that a few minutes earlier, the male therapist attacked him rather strongly with no response or reaction on his part. The topic of fear of authority figures arose, an issue that was a significant problem for the majority of the group members. With the aid of the female therapist, the patient was encouraged to express his hurt and resentment toward her colleague, which for him was a truly corrective emotional experience.

In the last meeting (the twentieth), at the request of the cotherapists, the patients started to give feedback regarding their group experience. The "leader" of the group described the group as a "hothouse," where she felt protected, was able to expose herself, share her intimate feelings and thoughts, and explore her inner conflicts and make changes in her behavior, as the dangers were small in comparison to the outside world. She felt that as a result of these "ideal" conditions, she grew and developed and was confident that she would be able to continue the process afterward.

Several other members shared similar feelings and bemoaned the fact that this was the last meeting. However, others took issue with this metaphor and spoke of their discomfort in the group, the pressures upon them, their difficulty in adapting to the group, and the minimal positive changes that took place in regard to their self-perception and behavior.

The male therapist at his turn, expressed the view that the group experience can be compared to a "laboratory" where a person has the opportunity to explore and experiment and learn about himself and others. The more a person invests and the greater effort he makes, the more he will get out of it.

The female therapist opined that she saw the group experience as a "hothouse" where "ideal" conditions are present for growth and where the plants are protected from the strong outside winds. In the hothouse there are present various species of plants and each grows and develops differently and at its own pace. Some grow taller and blossom, some strengthen their roots and thicken their stems, while others benefit by the hothouse in spite of the fact that they don't give an visible evidence of change. It is possible that the change will appear at a later time.

At this point, one of the members observed that the male therapist represented the "laboratory" in that throughout the meetings he consistently emphasized reality, change, and action. On the other hand, the female therapist represented the "hothouse" as she emphasized feelings, patience, support, and understanding.

Another member contributed that in his view the "laboratory" and "hothouse" provided the group members with an opportunity to be exposed to different aspects of themselves and others and a challenge to find an effective integration of the two.

16

Use of the TAT in Group Therapy with Children

SEYMOUR HOFFMAN, LEAH ROSMAN, AND AVIVA DANON

A therapeutic technique that combines Gardner's mutual storytelling technique (Gardner 1971) and the use of Thematic Apperception Test (TAT) cards using an active interactional co-therapy approach (Hoffman, et al., 1987 Chapter 1, this volume) with individual children was described in a recent publication (Hoffman and Wizansky 1989).

The advantage cited regarding this approach was the nonthreatening, playlike aspects of this technique, which circumvent the child's negativism and at the same time stimulates his interest and imagination and increases his involvement. In addition, since the focus of attention is on the "heroes" of the stories, highly emotionally laden and anxiety-provoking material can be introduced and discussed without frontally attacking the child's defensive structure.

A modification of this approach with groups of children developed by one of the authors (L. R.), was experimented with by cotherapists (S. H. and A. D.). The group consisted of six latency-age children, between the ages of 10 and 12, of divorced parents (or those who were in the process of divorce), who were referred to the clinic because of emotional and behavioral problems.

The goals of this brief but intensive group therapy program were to facilitate interaction and support among participants; promote recognition and understanding of emotions stemming from divorce; enable acceptance and working through of their loss, and confront and cope with problems arising from divorce; deal with family and peer relationships; develop positive self-image; and replace maladaptive behavior patterns with positive behaviors (Green 1978).

Treatment

An orientation meeting was held for the parents of the children referred to the clinic to explain to them the therapy program and enlist their cooperation. The parents were also informed that another parent group meeting would be held some time after termination of the program to share with them the therapists' views and impressions of their children and receive feedback from them regarding the effect of the group therapy experience on their children.

The children of the parents that expressed interest in the program and a willingness to cooperate were invited to a meeting with one of the psychologists, who administered selected cards of the TAT (Holt 1951) and explained to them the group therapy program.

After reviewing all the stories that the children related, the therapists selected one significant story of each child for presentation in the group meetings. In a collaborative effort, they prepared contrasting stories where the male therapist emphasized the "hero's" unacceptable impulses, thoughts and wishes, and maladaptive coping style, while his colleague emphasized the "hero's" strengths, flexibility, good judgment, and effective coping style.

At each of the six one-hour group meetings, one of the stories of the children was read while the respective TAT was displayed. This was followed by the "spontaneous" stories of the male and female therapists and an open, general group discussion. During the discussions, the therapists took an active part in raising and reacting to significant and relevant issues in a dialectical manner.

Following are excerpts of the first two meetings as recorded by a psychologist trainee who acted as an observer and recorder.

After an initial warm-up period, where the participants in the group shared some information about themselves with the other group members, the female therapist read the first story while her colleague displayed the appropriate TAT card to the children.

Card 8BM

In this card an adolescent boy looks straight out of the picture. The barrel of a rifle is visible at one side. In the background one can discern the dim scene of a surgical operation, like a reverie.

Child's Story

There was a boy whose father was in the army. He was wounded by a bullet and the boy was very sad. They took him to the hospital in order to find the bullet in him and this took many days. The boy in the meantime was sad and walked to the hospital to visit his father because there was no car. It took the doctors at least 10 days to find the bullet in him. The boy was happy that finally his father could return home. After they removed the bullet, the father screamed because of the pain. Afterward they put bandages on him and he went home. "How does the boy feel?" The boy feels good because his father returned home. "Home?" His parents are divorced. The boy lives with his mother but his father lives nearby. The boy sleeps at times at his mother's house and at times at his father's house.

Therapist's Story (S. H.)

The boy's father was wounded in a war and they brought him to the hospital for an operation. The boy is waiting outside the operating room and he has mixed feelings about what is going on. On the one hand, he is worried about his father and is concerned about his life. On the other hand, he feels that it serves his father right that he was wounded and is in pain because he is angry at him for leaving the family and getting divorced. The boy blames his father for not getting along with his mother and for not visiting him enough after the divorce. "How does the story end?" The father dies on the operating table and everyone pities the boy because he is an orphan.

Therapist's Story (A. D.)

Seymour, you exaggerate! Maybe the boy is angry that his father left the house but he doesn't wish the father to be dead.

I also see a father who was wounded and taken immediately to the hospital for an operation. The boy heard that his father was wounded and immediately went to the hospital because he was very concerned and worried about him and he wanted his father to know this, and that he loved him.

They operated on his father and the boy came every day to visit and take care of him in spite of the fact that he was angry at him. The boy felt that his father did not love him much since he left the house and went to live with another woman. He also didn't visit his son as frequently as he had promised.

"How does the story end?" The father recovered and returned to his house. However, he began to appreciate and understand his son's feelings and needs and became closer to him. The boy also better understood his father and became closer to him.

Card 3BM

On the floor against a couch is the huddled form of a figure with his head bowed on his right arm. Beside him on the floor is a revolver.

Child's Story

I see a boy. His bad mother put him in a room and locked him in so he couldn't get out. He was very sad and he began to cry near the clothes closet and he dried his tears with the clothes. He was very unhappy in the room alone. He wanted to be with his friends and he thought that his mother would not allow his friends to come into the room since she told them he was being punished.

In the end, mother allowed the children to enter the house and see that he was being punished. The friends said they wanted to play with him and the mother finally agreed to let them into the room. The children had a good time together.

Therapist's Story (S. H.)

A mother punished her child because she was fresh and did not behave well. She didn't permit her to leave the house and play with her friends.

Mother and child did not get along for several years, since the father had left home. The child blamed her mother for divorcing her father and at every opportunity she nagged her to let him return to the family. When nagging didn't help, the child began wetting her bed at night, became disrespectful, cursed and screamed at her mother, started fights in school and at home, and didn't do her homework. In this way, the child tried to show her mother that she was angry at her, missed her father and wanted her to let him return home.

"How does the story end?" The mother finally gave in and permitted the father to return home.

Therapist's Story (A. D.)

Seymour, do you really think that a child can force parents to return to live together? The reason they separated was because they stopped loving each other, didn't get along and even hated each other at times.

I have another story.

Mother punished her child because she misbehaved. She did this because she wanted to teach her to be a polite, likable, and successful person who gets along well with her family and friends.

The mother understood that her child was angry about the divorce and it was very difficult for her to accept and adjust to the situation, since she missed her father very much. However, she felt that she had to accept and adapt to reality. At times when the mother sensed that her daughter was angry or sad about the situation, she tried to talk to her and help her understand her feelings and solve her problems. When the mother felt that she wasn't able to help her daughter, she decided to consult a psychologist together with the child. In the discussions with the psychologist, the child began to understand that by misbehaving she was expressing her anger toward her parents and was trying to punish them. She slowly recognized that she wasn't responsible for their divorce and that there was no way that she could reunite them, since the parents stopped loving each other. She began to talk about her feelings to her parents and gradually understood and accepted the situation.

Group Discussion (Excerpts from the Two Meetings)

S. H.: Aviva, don't you think that the boy is very angry at his father for leaving the family and wishes that bad things would happen to him?

A. D.: I agree that the boy is angry at his father and it could be that he is also angry at his mother. But the boy still loves his father and wants to continue to see and be with him. He doesn't want him to die.

S. H.: I'm sure the boy has not forgiven his father for getting divorced and living with another woman.

A. D.: I think the boy understands that the parents divorced because they stopped loving each other and not because of him or because of selfish reasons.

S. H.: I'm sure there are children in this group who agree with me.

Dan: I'm not angry at my father. I don't wish him bad things.

Sam: I'm a little angry at my father, especially when he doesn't visit when he promises.

Ann: I want both my parents to be well and happy. My father remarried and his wife is pregnant. I hope it's a boy.

Ron: I'm not angry. I now have two fathers. My father buys me toys when he visits.

Fay: My father at times disappears from the house for several days after a fight. But he always returns.

A. D.: Do you worry at times that he may never return?

Fay: No. I'd rather they stay together even though they fight sometimes.

Joe: I'm glad my parents divorced. Now there's peace in the house.

S. H.: I would think that it must be difficult for you children to concentrate in school because of the family problems. I would expect that you also have problems getting along with your friends and parents.

Joe: Sometimes I wonder when my father will return home and I don't pay attention to the teacher.

Dan: I don't have any problems.

Ron: Sometimes I misbehave when my father doesn't visit me or doesn't bring me a present.

Sam: Sometimes I break things at home when I'm angry at my mother. I threaten to run away from home and go live with my father.

S. H.: How many children still hope that their fathers will return home? (Several children answered in the affirmative.)

S. H.: I bet some of you misbehave or nag your mothers so that your parents will agree to live together.

A. D.: Do you think that a child really believes that he could cause his parents to live together after years of not getting along? Everyone suffered in the past. Why should they want to suffer again?

Toward the end of the discussion periods, the male therapist began softening his position and gradually "saw" the merits of his colleague's viewpoints.

At the conclusion of each meeting the female therapist summarized the discussions and encouraged the children to return for the next meeting.

In the remaining group meetings, the therapists, using the same format, were able to raise and focus on other sensitive and pertinent issues and topics with the children and succeeded in stimulating their active participation in the sessions.

A follow-up meeting with the parents of the children was scheduled two weeks after the last group session. All the mothers attended and participated actively in the meeting. Several mothers reported some positive changes in their children's behavior. One mother spoke of the greater openness on the part of her child, while another mentioned that she received a picture of a dove for a present with the inscription, "To mother who always makes peace in the family."

Another mother complained that her daughter is still very closed but was surprised that for the first time her daughter asked questions about the divorce.

Two mothers reported improvement in their children's behavior in school but not at home.

The parents expressed great interest in knowing what transpired in the meetings, but because of the issue of confidentiality they were provided only with the general impressions of the therapists.

There was general agreement that further work was required and various possible formats were discussed, such as continued group therapy for the children, parent group meetings, or a combination of both.

A final decision was postponed until after the holiday recess.

Conclusion

Initially the children were fearful and reticent in sharing their feelings and thoughts and much denial, evasiveness, and caution were evident in their behavior.

However, gradually, with the provocative behavior on the part of one of the therapists and the supportive behavior on the part of the other, the children were able to loosen up and participate in the group meetings.

The presence of other children "being in the same boat" seemed to have a liberating effect on the children, who were able to give expression to their pent-up feelings, pain, conflicts, and fears.

The majority of the children seemed to enjoy identifying with and supporting the views of the "positive" female therapist against those of her colleague.

It was the therapists' impression that use of the TAT stories as a stimulus for discussion and the cotherapists' approach facilitated and stimulated openness and active participation on the part of the children.

References

Gardner, R. A. (1971). *Therapeutic Communication with Children: The Mutual Storytelling Technique*. New York: Science House.

Green, B. J. (1978). Helping children of divorce: A multi-modal approach. *Elementary School Guidance and Counseling* 12:31–45.

Hoffman, S., Kohener, R., and Shapira, M. (1987). Two in one: Dialectical psychotherapy. *Psychotherapy* 24(2):212–216.

Hoffman, S., and Wizansky, B. (1989). Brief therapeutic intervention using a modified storytelling technique. *International Journal of Short-Term Psychotherapy* 4:189–194.

Holt, R. (1951). The thematic aperception test. In: *An Introduction to Projective Techniques*, ed. R. Holt, and G. L. Anderson. Englewood Cliffs, NJ: Prentice-Hall.

17

Teaching Cotherapy

SARAH GAFNI AND SEYMOUR HOFFMAN

In working with many cotherapists over the last ten years in treating individuals, couples, families, and groups, we have become convinced that cotherapy significantly adds to the complexity, richness, flexibility, brevity, and effectiveness of the therapeutic process and also to the professional development of the therapist (Hoffman and Gafni 1984, Chapter 2, this volume).

Recently, we conducted a course on cotherapy for our colleagues at the mental health center where we are employed. The course consisted of readings and discussions of selected articles (Dick et al. 1980, Gafni et al. 1990, Chapter 12, this volume, Hoffman et al. 1987, Chapter 1, this volume; from a reader on cotherapy (Hoffman et al. 1990), role playing, various exercises to increase self-awareness and sensitivity, live demonstrations of cotherapy treatment by the authors, and supervision of cases treated by the cotherapists who participated in the course.

The first meeting was devoted to an open discussion of the expectations of the participants of the course, their concepts and experiences with cotherapy, and an outline of the course and the assigned reading material for future discussions.

Topics and issues raised in this and subsequent meetings included the advantages and disadvantages of cotherapy, when is cotherapy the treatment of choice, selecting cotherapists, relationship between cotherapists, and difficulties and problems that may arise between cotherapists.

Considerable attention and discussion were devoted to cotherapy factors that produce success (Roller and Nelson 1991), such as (1) complementary balance of skills, (2) compatibility of theoretical viewpoints, (3) openness in communication, (4) equality of participation, (5) mutual liking, and (6) mutual respect.

Interspersed between the theoretical discussions were specific exercises to increase the participants' awareness and sensitivity in selecting and working with cotherapists.

In one exercise the group was asked to describe and list their personality traits on a piece of paper, and on the other side of the page, the attributes that they sought and valued in their cotherapist. Afterward, the participants paired off and exchanged ideas with several of the group members regarding their ideal cotherapist.

A general discussion was then held in which the students shared what they learned about themselves, about others, and about their expectations from their cotherapist.

The similarity between selecting an ideal mate and ideal cotherapist was noted and discussed, as well as issues dealing with mutual trust, competition, compromise, cooperation, flexibility, and complementary and symmetrical relationships.

Another exercise that the group participated in was the simultaneous hand movement exercise, in which the partners touched palms and moved their hands in a free and undirected fashion. After two minutes elapsed, one of the partners directed the movement for two minutes, and afterward the other partner took charge for the same amount of time. After repeating the exercise with several different partners, the group discussed their experiences and related them to issues of power struggle, competition, and cooperation.

Several meetings were devoted to live demonstrations of cotherapy by the instructors with a family, a couple, and an individual patient. The patients, who were in treatment with several of the participants, were chosen because of their intractability to therapeutic intervention and their willingness to appear in front of a group of professionals.

Prior to each meeting with the clients, the cotherapists, in the presence of the group, devoted some time to discussing between themselves the upcoming case and exchanging ideas about possible issues to focus on and the kinds of interventions and roles each would undertake during the session.

Following the session, the cotherapists again spent some time exchanging views and providing feedback to each other regarding their impressions of the meeting.

In the discussions that followed the demonstrations, the group related to the cotherapy interactions and especially to the mutual support, synchronization, and open communication that was evidenced throughout the sessions by the cotherapists.

One participant compared the cotherapy intervention to doubles play in tennis, where at times the partners play net, at times back court, and at times one partner plays net and the other back court.

In following meetings, the group participated in role-playing exercises in which several members simulated a troubled family, couple, and individual patient, while two participants played the role of cotherapists. The "cotherapists" also exchanged ideas and provided feedback to each other in the presence of the group, before and after their "therapeutic intervention." This was followed by feedback and general discussion by the group.

The last few sessions were devoted primarily to supervision of cotherapy cases treated by the group members. Issues and problems brought to supervision included personality conflicts, competition, and lack of trust and open communication between cotherapists. One point that was emphasized was the importance of pre-and posttherapy discussions between cotherapists.

The last meeting of the sixteen-session course was devoted to a general discussion of the course with the aid of a brief questionnaire that the participants had filled out the previous week.

Following is a sample of the comments and responses of the participants:

"This learning experience enabled me to be familiar with a new therapeutic approach and appreciate its usefulness and effectiveness in certain cases and situations. It seems fascinating and appealing, but I feel I have to deepen my knowledge and experience, since it is quite complicated and demanding and can cause problems and difficulties."

"I definitely see the value of cotherapy in working with groups, families, and couples. With individual patients, never."

"I enjoyed the experience in working with another therapist. I learned about myself and my difficulty in sharing control and responsibility."

"Cotherapy is a highly effective way to learn to do therapy when working with an experienced therapist."

At the request of the group, it was decided to continue to hold weekly group supervisory sessions on cotherapy after conclusion of the course.

Conclusion

Cotherapy as Keith and Whitaker (1983) describe it, "is a specialized technique in the art of psychotherapy" (p. 91). It is our feeling that this form of treatment should be taught to clinicians from all disciplines, in order to add to their therapeutic armamentarium an effective, dynamic method of treating individuals, couples, families, and groups.

References

Dick, B., Lessler, K., and Whiteside, J. (1980). A developmental framework for cotherapy. *International Journal of Group Psychotherapy* 30(30): 273–285.

Gafni, S., Laub, B., and Lavie, Y. (1991). "Challenging" therapist–"supportive" therapist: a model of therapeutic intervention with anorectic families. *Family Therapy* 17(3).

Hoffman, S., and Gafni, S. (1984). Active interactional cotherapy. *International Journal of Family Therapy* 6(1):53–58.

Hoffman, S., Kohener, R., and Shapira, M. (1987). Two on one: dialectical psychotherapy. *Psychotherapy* 24:212–216.

Keith, D. V. and Whitaker, C. A. (1983), Cotherapy with families. In *Handbook of Family and Marital Therapy*, ed. B. B. Wolman and G. Stricker, p. 91. New York: Plenum.

Roller, B., and Nelson, V. (1991). *The Art of Cotherapy: How Therapists Work Together.* New York: Guilford.

Rubinstein, D. (1981). Cotherapy: rationale, dynamics and techniques. Is two better than one? In *Group and Family Therapy*, ed. R. Wohlberg, and M. Aronson. New York: Brunner/Mazel.

Credits

Chapter 7: Originally published in the *American Journal of Psychotherapy*, vol. 45, no. 2, April 1992. Copyright © 1991 by the Association for the Advancement of Psychotherapy and reprinted with permission.

Chapter 8: Originally published in the *International Journal of Short-Term Therapy*, vol. 9, no. 4, October 1994. Copyright © 1994 by John Wiley & Sons Ltd. and reprinted with permission.

Chapter 9: Originally published in the *International Journal of Short-Term Therapy*, vol. 9, no. 1, January 1994. Copyright © 1994 by John Wiley & Sons Ltd. and reprinted with permission.

Chapter 10: Originally published in *Contemporary Family Therapy*, vol. 8, no. 2, Summer 1986. Copyright © 1986 by Human Sciences Press and reprinted by permission of Plenum Publishing Corp.

Chapter 11: Originally published in *Family Therapy*, vol. 14, no. 1. Copyright © 1987 by Libra Publishing Inc. and reprinted by permission.

Chapter 12: Originally published in *Family Therapy*, vol. 17, no. 3. Copyright © 1990 by Libra Publishing Inc. and reprinted by permission.

Chapter 13: Originally published in *Family Therapy*, vol. 17, no. 2. Copyright © 1990 by Libra Publishing Inc. and reprinted by permission.

Chapter 14: Originally published in *Family Therapy*, vol. 16, no. 3. Copyright © 1989 by Libra Publishing Inc. and reprinted by permission.

Chapter 15: Originally published in the *Journal of Group Psychotherapy*, vol. 39, no. 3, July 1989. Copyright © 1989 by The Guilford Press and reprinted with permission.

Chapter 16: Originally published in the *Journal of Child and Adolescent Group Therapy*, vol. 3, no. 2. Copyright © 1993 by Human Sciences Press and reprinted by permission of Plenum Publishing Corp.

Chapter 17: Originally published in the *Journal of Contemporary Psychotherapy*, vol. 21, no. 4. Copyright © 1991 by Human Sciences Press and reprinted by permission of Plenum Publishing Corp.

Index

Active-interactional cotherapy, 15–20. *See also* Cotherapy
Adelman, M. B., 103
Adler, A., x
Anorexia nervosa. *See* Anorexic families; Bulimarexic disorders
Anorexic families, 109–120. *See also* Bulimarexic disorders
  case discussions, 116–119
  case illustrations, 112–116
  literature on treatment for, 109–110
  therapeutic process, 110–112

Bemis, K. M., 109
Bernard, H. S., xiii, 59, 64
Berne, E., 71
Bootzin, R., 77
Borderline patient, 21–33
  case study, 22–33
    description of patient, 22–24
    treatment, 24–33
  overview of, 21–22
Boscolo, L., 111
Boskind-Lodahl, M., 35
Breit, M., 124
Browne, E., 90
Bruch, H., 109, 110, 117
Bulimarexic disorders, 35–43. *See also* Anorexic families
  case illustration, 36–42
    description of patient, 36–37
    family involvement, 39
    negative transference, 41
    patient improvement, 40–41
    rationale for cotherapy approach, 37
    sexual molestation, 39–40
    termination, 41–42
    therapist functioning, 37–39
  overview of, 35–36

Caille, P., 109
Campbell, R. J., 89
Collinson, S., 3
Consultants, 79–85
  case discussions, 84–85
  case illustrations, 80–84
    depression, 80–82
    obsessional thinking, 82–84
  overview of use of, 79–80

Cooper-Haber, K., xiv, 129
Cotherapists, characteristics required of, 15–16
Cotherapy, 3–13
  active-interactional cotherapy, 15–20. *See also* Active-interactional cotherapy
  as adjunct therapy, 3
  advantages and benefits of, xiii, 3, 4, 15
  with borderline patient, 21–33. *See also* Borderline patient
  bulimarexic disorders, 35–43. *See also* Bulimarexic disorders
  case illustrations
    depression, 5–9
    encopresis, 20
    juvenile delinquency, 18–20
    learning difficulties, 9–12
    marital relations, 17–18, 20
  consultants, 79–85. *See also* Consultants
  described, xiii
  family cotherapy. *See* Family cotherapy
  group cotherapy. *See* Group cotherapy
  history of, x
  iatrogenically infantilized patient, 65–72. *See also* Iatrogenically infantilized patient
  overview of, 3–5
  patient profile for, 3–4
  phantom cotherapist, 57–64. *See also* Phantom cotherapist
  phobias, 73–78. *See also* Phobias
  process in, xiv, 5, 16
  teaching of, 149–152
  Thematic Apperception Test (TAT) card use, 45–56, 141–148. *See also* Thematic Apperception Test cards
  time frame and, xiii–xiv
Countertransference, cotherapy and, 15
Crisp, A. H., 35

Danon, A., 141
Depression
  consultants, case illustrations, 80–82
  individual cotherapy, case illustration, 5–9
  phantom cotherapist, 57–64. *See also* Phantom cotherapist
de Shazer, S., xiv, 110
Diamond, R. E., 99
Dick, B., 149
Dowling, E., 130
Dryud, J. E., 3
Dym, B., 109

Elective mutism, 89–97
  age at onset, 89–90
  case discussion, 95–96
  case study, 91–95
  defined, 89
  groupings of, 89
  therapeutic approaches to, 90
Elson, A., 90
Encopresis, cotherapy, case illustration, 20
Eron, J. B., 121

Family cotherapy
  anorexic families, 109–120. *See also* Anorexic families
  elective mutism, 89–97. *See also* Elective mutism

marital cotherapy, 129–134. *See also* Marital cotherapy
"marital phobias," 121–127. *See also* "Marital phobias"
"matricide" case illustration, 99–107. *See also* "Matricide" case
Family dynamics
bulimarexic disorders, case illustration, 39
cotherapy and, 15
"matricide" case, 100–101
Thematic Apperception Test (TAT) cards (case illustration), 45–49
Family therapy, cotherapy and, x, xiv
Feedback, cotherapy and, 15
Fishman, H. C., 118
Framo, J. L., 4
Frances, A., 65, 72
Friedman, R., 89

Gafni, S., xiii, xv, 5, 38, 96, 102, 110, 149
Gans, R. W., 15
Gardner, R. A., 141
Garfinkel, P. E., 109
Garner, D. M., 109
Goldfried, M. R., 109
Gorkin, M., 64
Green, B. J., 142
Greiver, D., 15
Grinker, R. R., Sr., 21
Group cotherapy, x, 137–152
case study of college students in, 137–140
teaching of, 149–152
Thematic Apperception Test (TAT) cards, 141–148
case discussion, 148
overview of, 141–142
treatment, 142–148
Guerin, P. J., 47

Haber, R., xiv, 129
Haley, J., 117, 121
Halmi, K., 109
Heilfron, M., xiii, 16
Held, B. S., 22, 37
Hinsie, L. E., 89
Hoffman, S., xiii, xiv, xv, 5, 24, 36, 37, 38, 57, 68, 80, 84, 85, 96, 102, 103, 110, 129, 141, 149
Holt, M., 15
Holt, R., 142
Hudson, J. I., 35

Iatrogenically infantilized patient, 65–72
case study, 66–67
overview, 65
treatment process, 67–71
Identification, cotherapy and, 15
Individual cotherapy. *See* Cotherapy
Individual therapy, cotherapy and, 3, 4
Interpersonal relationships, cotherapy and, 15

Jehu, D., 90
Juvenile delinquency, cotherapy, case illustration, 18–20

Kalucy, R. S., 109
Karagan, N., 89
Kaufman, M., 117
Keith, D. V., 79, 84, 152
Kernberg, O. F., 21

L'Abate, L. A., 69, 70
Laub, B., 5, 37, 57, 103, 110
Learning difficulties, individual cotherapy, case illustration, 9–12
Lick, J., 77
Lindblad, M. B., 89, 90

MacLennan, B., 15
Madanes, C., 123
Mari, S., 103
Marital cotherapy, 129–134
  case discussion, 134
  case illustration, 130–134
  overview of, 129–130
"Marital phobias," 121–127. *See also* Phobias
  background, 122
  case discussion, 125–126
  presenting problem, 121–122
  treatment, 122–125
Marital relations, cotherapy, case illustration, 17–18, 20
"Matricide" case, 99–107
  family sessions, 102–103
  follow-up, 107
  individual sessions, 103–106
  patient history and family background, 100–101
  presenting problems, 99–100
  treatment, 101–102
McGee, T. F., 15, 16
Meijer, A., 90
Merdler, A., 57, 129
Millman, H. L., 22
Mintz, E. E., 24
Minuchin, S., 35, 102, 109, 112, 117, 118
Mirroring, cotherapy and, 16
Modeling, cotherapy and, 16
Mora, C., 90
Moreno, J., x
Morrison, D. A. R., 12, 37, 110
Morrison, J. K., 123
Mullan, H., 4

Napier, A., 15
Negative transference, bulimarexic disorders, case illustration, 41
Nelson, V., 22, 150
Nolan, J., 90
Nunnelly, K. G., 4

O'Connell, D. S., 67, 123, 125
Omer, H., xiv, 118

Papp, P., xiv, 63, 80, 110
Pence, C., 90
Pendagast, E. F., 47
Penn, P., 105
Phantom cotherapist, 57–64
  case discussion, 63–64
  case report, 57–63
Phobias, 73–78. *See also* "Marital phobias"
  case discussion, 77–78
  overview, 73
  patient description, 74
  treatment process, 74–77
Piaget, G. W., 3
Piaget, J., 52
Polivy, J., 35
Pope, H. G., 35

Rabin, H. M., 15
Reid, W. H., 22, 73
Resistance, cotherapy and, 17
Rioch, M. J., 3
Rohrbaugh, M., 121
Roller, B., 22, 150

Rosenberg, B. J., 89, 90
Rubinstein, D., xiii
Russell, A., xiii
Russell, L., xiii
Ruzicka, B., 90

Sackin, H., 90
Sadeh, T., 117
Sanguiliano, I., 4
Sargent, J., 109, 112
Schizophrenia, cotherapy for, 4
Schuman, B. N., 15, 16
Segal, H., 80, 85
Segal, S., 129
Seltzer, M. R., 104
Seltzer, W. J., 104
Selvini-Palazzoli, M., 109, 111
Serber, M., 3
Sexual molestation, bulimarexic disorders, case illustration, 39–40
Sheinberg, M., xiv, 110
Silver, D., 22
Sluckin, A., 90
Solomon, A. P., 12, 37, 110
Sours, J. A., 35
Stunkard, A., 35
Suicide
  "matricide" case illustration, 99–107. *See also* "Matricide" case
  phantom cotherapist, 57–64. *See also* Phantom cotherapist
Supervision, cotherapy and, 15

Termination, bulimarexic disorders, case illustration, 41–42
Thematic Apperception Test (TAT) cards (case illustration), 45–56
  case discussion, 55–56
  family background and history, 45–49
  patient's response to therapist's stories, 50–53
  patient's story, 49, 53–55
  presenting problem, 45
  psychologist's story, 49–50
  social worker's story, 50
Thematic Apperception Test (TAT) cards (group cotherapy), 141–148
  case discussion, 148
  overview of, 141–142
  treatment, 142–148
Therapeutic impasse, consultant intervention for, 79–85. *See also* Consultants
Therapeutic relationship, flexibility in, ix–x, 99
Torrey, E., 126
Transference
  cotherapy and, 15
  negative, bulimarexic disorders, case illustration, 41
Trauma, cotherapy for, 45–56. *See also* Thematic Apperception Test cards (case illustration)
Travers, J. A., 65
Treppa, J. A., xv, 4, 5, 41

Watterson, D. J., 3
Weeks, G. R., 69, 70
Whitaker, C. A., 3, 15, 79, 84, 152
White, M., 109
Wizansky, B., 141
Wright, H. L., 90